"Sometimes a poem commands us to sit down and stop talking and listen. We do. We recognize, as if through gauze the figure being revealed, a person here who tastes life and finds it good and swallows grief and does not know what to do but does not leave us alone. This person wants to share life … I read 'Homecoming' and I stand at attention. [Christine Van Brunt] create[s] fables and make[s] them real and give[s] them titles. 'Safe Deposit' 'Annals of Love' 'Lies of You Know Who.' Some of them are complete as a soldier dressed to go to war. Some of them are fascinating tatters, the traces someone has left on a kitchen counter."

—Richard Loomis, Ph.D
Professor Emeritus of English Literature
Nazareth College of Rochester

"Christine Van Brunt's poems resonate with the seasons, plunge and soar through landmark events, and illuminate the 'divine in the ordinary.' We heartily recommend this collection to all who hunger and thirst for the surprises and presence of God."

—Virgil and Lynn Nelson,
American Baptist Pastor and
Missionary Couple

"In her poems Christine Van Brunt shines a bright, insight-filled light on the "Toe Holds" she and we share in our lives. A thoughtful observer of both the outside world and her own inner experience, she puts meaning to the 'stop and smell the roses' sentiment. The reader of her poetry is likely to re-experience the everyday and special moments of life with new perspective. Family, friends, self and even bugs may be seen more clearly than before. To experience life a moment at a time, here is a manual. Stop a moment and enjoy."

—Richard Arnold, Ph.D.
Clinical Psychologist

"Christy's poems reflect human nature, and the divinity inherent within human nature. Layers of meaning are unveiled as the reader experiences the beautiful simplicity. What a treat!"

—Patti Cook
Energy Therapist

"In simple, straightforward words, Christy Van Brunt describes daily experiences that fulfill her sense of mission to encourage and lift the spirits of ordinary readers. Her love for her resilient, soft-spoken husband, the joys of motherhood and walks at dawn, a son's return from the war, pollination, clean sheets, vivid metaphors of water and snow, and the struggle to balance self-affirmation and awareness of one's limits: these moments reveal 'the warm heart of the universe beating underneath the dark.'"

—Hugh Barbour
Professor Emeritus of History of Religion
and Bible Earlham College

toe

holds

in the

LIGHT

toe

holds

in the

LIGHT

Poems to Navigate
the Fullness of
Human Experience

Christine Van Brunt

TATE PUBLISHING & *Enterprises*

Published by Tate Publishing & Enterprises, LLC
127 E. Trade Center Terrace | Mustang, Oklahoma 73064 USA
1.888.361.9473 | www.tatepublishing.com

Tate Publishing is committed to excellence in the publishing industry. The company reflects the philosophy established by the founders, based on Psalm 68:11,
"The Lord gave the word and great was the company of those who published it."

Book design copyright © 2011 by Tate Publishing, LLC. All rights reserved.
Cover design by Leah LeFlore
Interior design by Nathan Harmony

Published in the United States of America

ISBN: 978-1-61739-364-8
1. Poetry: General
2. Poetry: Inspirational & Religious
11.01.03

For my husband, Nicholas

Table of Contents

Foreword

What's in it for you if you read this book?

This book offers a way of seeing. Sometimes that way of seeing will jive with your perceptions; sometimes it will challenge them. Sometimes it will illuminate things you didn't even know were there.

While poems are the medium, *seeing* is the subject. *Seeing* assumes *light*; the one is impossible without the other. So by inference, this book is also about *the light*. It explores not only *what we see*, but also *how we see it*, the lenses we use, the *emotional film* on which we record our experiences, the compositions and interpretations we make.

There is honesty on every page.

Nothing is too small for our scrutiny; anything can make an impact.

Testifying to blinding beauty all the way, and sometimes to crippling or rocket-launching emotion, the book looks into your perceptual cracks and crevices, frog kicks through oceans, hangs suspended over chasms, scales walls, belays up rock faces, and stands in rapture at summits. It finds, snaps word pictures, and "outs" what is there in the whole human climb toward clarity.

Preface

The impulse to create art—what is it? Is it the need to make order out of something disorderly? Is it the need to make meaning out of something chaotic? Is it the need to make beauty out of something painful? Is it the need to pour out thanks for something so glorious it hurts?

For me it is the need to get something expressed that is intensely lived or felt: to get that thing into words—to preserve it—whether only for the first blush of understanding or for a recurring impulse to do further study. For whatever reasons, it can be returned to again and again, and kept, and found, and used. It is the way I process—make sense of—raw emotion. I am both impelled to do it the way a hungry man must eat, and overjoyed to do it the way a gourmand loves exquisite dining.

How do my poems come to be?

They come in a myriad of ways. Sometimes a poem is a surprise, blooming on the brow like a volunteer flower. Sometimes it starts as an annoyance, like a weed in the flowerbed, goading me into rooting it out, and then resisting expulsion like the most pernicious vining root in the garden, veering off in so unknown and ranging a course that I can only get the whole thing by unearthing the yard. Sometimes it just climbs into the heart and incubates, and then sometime later—maybe days, maybe years—climbs out again, fully formed like a mature butterfly emerging whole from its chrysalis. And sometimes I just so ache to say it, and it is so deeply embedded in and inextricably connected throughout my consciousness, that finding the words seems as hard as pulling arteries out of the very flesh and organs that stick to them, out of the living tissue they entwine and feed.

Sometimes, for me, there is nothing more painful than writing poetry, except not writing it. Sometimes, for me, there is nothing more exhilarating than writing poetry, except the thing that it is about, which is why I must write it.

Knock, Knock

Awakening

Tasks ambush you, and tie you up,
And put a blindfold o'er your eyes
And so you work, n'er looking up
Missing out on many a surprise.

Then one moment Wonder frees you
And takes the blindfold from your eyes;
Beauty then begins to feed you,
And now you see and you are wise.

Cold Remedy

On the other side of the Cold—
Is the great warm Heart
Of the Universe
Beating

Everywhere behind
And underneath
The Dark—
Is Life Gestating

Preparing to
Break out into
Spring

Never mind the solstice

You can have
That great
Awakening
Any time

It is always there

On the other side of the Cold—
Is the great warm Heart
Of the Universe
Beating

Come Out and Play

Wander Awhile

Wander awhile in my mind with me.
Take off your shoes and unloose your hair.
Hear the voice of the honey bee.
Wander awhile in my mind with me.

Romp for a while in my mind with me.
Swoop from the path, and scoop up the hills.
Hold armloads of flowers, hear earfuls of rills
Hug all the grass and climb every tree
Romp for a while in my mind with me.

Slip for a while through my mind with me.
Shallowly breathe, glide silently.
Shy beasts—wondrous—may share thy space
Stand stock still right in your place.
Stand stock still before their grace.
A buck has paused. He holds your eye:
In this moment … Infinity.

Who quivers most? Is it he? Is it I?
Hold your breath long as he stands by.
Then—A snort, a stamp, a breath ere he fly
And where he was—but a steam and a sigh …
Slip for a while through my mind with me.

Wonder's Promise

As the rain soaks the earth
As the sun wakes the seed
As the leaf seeks the light
As the blade parts the soil
As the bud heaves the mud
As the day breaks the bloom
As the bee combs the flower
As the wind trembles the tree

That's how much Life loves you
That's how much Life loves me

Things That Fill

On a lovely day,
Walking outside can surpass
Eating and drinking.

A beautiful sky
Can nourish the hungry soul
More, even, than thinking.

Open Up

Those half-lidded eyes, open up
Overhead are skidding skies, open up
Wake from your slumber in the sun; fill your cup.

Light-Shows
That Rock

Old Spruces

Each green spruce needle
Glistens with sunlight along
The whole swaying branch,

And—flanked by its kin—
Forms a bright fringe on each graceful
Tendril of tree.

Long wands—so gently
Stirred by each finger of wind—
Bow, lift, and beckon.

A prettier thing
I never saw. Whole trees sigh
And shudder, whisper

And shift, their siren
Boughs luring me in, 'til I—
I am utterly—

Shipwrecked in awe.

Old Man Winter
is a Woman

That love child of Mother Earth
And Father Skies—Beauty—

Traipses freely around the planet
With her closet full of clothes,
And never wears the same thing twice.

In our little stretch of the world
There were these eye-witness reports:

Monday, she wore mother-of-pearl—
Pinked as in a kitten's ears.

Tuesday, she twirled into town
In a silver kimono, brushing faces
With her long sleeves, when she wasn't
Trailing them along the ground.

Wednesday, she tip-toed in
Wearing silk-screen snows, and
Softly shook out slanting sleet that
Silvered all the trees.

Thursday, her discarded flannel skirts
Lay in voluptuous disarray,
Flung onto rooftops, strewn in the streets,
Fanned out over every field.

Friday, she wore blue shadows
Morning and night, and in between,
Stood motionless, wearing only
Sequined light.

Saturday, she wore sheerest ice and
Tinkled everywhere she walked.
And Sunday's golden fleece in the morning
Was exchanged for gray wool in the afternoon.

So goes one week's inventory of
She Who Is Everywhere.

Whenever I catch a glimpse of her, I stop—
And, though I was taught better, I gulp—
And so help me God, I stare.

On the Blue Formica

On the blue Formica are
Clumps of cottage cheese.
A thinning fringe of table runner
Fraying fiber leaves.

Iridescent mashed potatoes,
Tapioca in a mound,
Soft froth of boiled frosting—
Are scattered all around!

"Who ate here and left this mess?"
Perplexed, I ask aloud.
"Who left upon this clean, blue sky
Such untidy piles of cloud?"

Riding through the Rain

Deep in my car, safe in my lane,
I see silver lasers pinpoint the grain
Of the shining pavement slicked by the rain
Unrolling like ribbon from a silver skein.

Head against plush seat, I love to hear
The tiny fingers tapping the car,
While the whispering tires wick away wet,
And the engine's vibration purrs like a cat.

I know this comfort, like memories I keep.
Like a rocking chair, it lulls me to sleep.
Like a ticking clock, it slowly repeats.
Like a loving lap, it is familiar and deep.

Combustion

The sun is out—Sing! Shout!
Buds are swelling 'round about;
Lassies are lean, and laddies stout;
The sun, the sun, the sun is out!

Birdies preen with a bright eye,
Go gadding about a gladsome sky.
And squirrels combust in yards and trees,
Up and down trunks like bushy-tailed bees.

And newborn lambs gambol in glee
—Fluff on legs in a grassy sea.
And the sea is turning from drab to green,
So tune up your eye and make it keen!

The sun is out—Sing! Shout!
April's arrived—Shy Spring will out!
And we'll ne'er more have a reason to pout,
The sun, the sun, the sun is out!

Water

Water, water, bubbling bright,
Filling earth with sound and light,

Crystal clear yet strangely soft,
You can bear most things aloft.

Nothing stops you, big or small,
You can wend your way through all,

Flowing over stepping stones,
Cutting canyons to their bones

Quenching all with purest strength
Cleansing all along your length

All the way unto the sea
Springing forth in greenery

Water, water, bubbling bright,
Embrace the earth with pliant might.

I Followed Spring

I followed Spring, to spy on her.
It was not a slender sylph I saw,
Hiding in shadow, blushing,
Dropping violets as she
Fleeted away…

It was a fat, yellow ball of sunshine,
Who got in my face!
And then took the fields
With a flying tackle,
Spilling all his golden
Bulk upon the ground…

Who knew Spring was so buff a boy
—All energy and splendor—
Body Builder,
Sprinter, Athlete,
A beefy tackle who can't
Be outrun?

Cumulous Clouds
in a Stiff Wind

Overhead go the white steeds,
Muscles bunched and armor gleaming,
Silent thunder as they fly,
Haunches strong and mane streaming.

Overhead go the white steeds,
Boiling power on the hoof,
Heads high and nostrils flaring,
Roiling, kingly, and aloof.

Overhead go the white steeds,
Tackle glinting as they pass,
Carrying archers whose bows are sewing
Silver arrows in the grass.

The Thief

Stunning is the tree in his lush greenery,
And a more cunning thief you'll never find!
He rips off the sunshine right before your eyes,
And plays the subtlest tricks on your mind.

Lolling in his wealth, he swaggers overhead,
Bragging of his haul with reckless ease:
He flaunts it, and shifts it, assuming you won't see,
And hides his shining loot in his leaves.

Toe Holds in the Light

Someone Took a Feathered Brush

Someone took a feathered brush,
applied it to the sky,
Gave the wash of palest blush a smoky tracery,

Touched a match of molten rose
to phantom pewter wisps
That stretched their paws and slipped
away in shades of amethyst,

Painted in the twilit hush bold
canyons—slate and blue
Then braided them with lava streams
that flashed, then passed from view.

Christine Van Brunt

Dawning

The front door creaks, out I peep;
Rabbits in shadow munch grasses in the dew.
Robins in the dawn breakfast on the lawn,
And the sky brightens bit by bit from indigo to blue.

With all his might, the Sun hurls light,
Wakes the morning glories drowsing on the trellis,
Splashes all the trees with star-shine bright,
Shows off so much that the Moon gets jealous.

On my front step I wait, replete,
Watching as the heavens turn forget-me-not blue.
The hope is high and the peace is deep,
And then around the corner comes shining you.

The Ballet

Is it just trees, this bobbing ballet?
The poplars—like dancers—
Stand in a row, just so—
Long necked and poised,
Their rounded arms
Playing tag with the air,
Which, brimming, lets
Itself get caught, then
Makes a mock show
Of breaking free and
Skimming away.

The poplars—attired
Head to toe in leaf sequins,
Set the stage aglow
In a whole shivering affair
Which is seldom still.

Christine Van Brunt

Like dancers—the trees
Bend and bow; in each
Teasing breeze their leaves
Quiver and shift; in fact
They steal the show.

Each pivots: To fro,
To fro, to fro, to fro,
To fro, on its tether

With the twirling,
Reverse twirling
Purling current of a
Breeze-driven meter.

And who is the light crew
For this spectacular show?

None other than Apollo.

Sky Limerick

Oh, filmy spring cloud up on high,
Methinks you do the Sun defy!
Its scattered golden beams you gather,
Bleach them in your whitest lather,
Then hang them billowing to dry—
Silver sheets across the sky.

Oh filmy spring cloud, seeming shy
Methinks you are a wee bit sly!
Where Sun had streaked the sky with gold,
You squeeze it through your whitest fold,
And make a mist of silver spray,
And then the whole sky overlay.

Oh filmy spring cloud, spanning space,
Methinks you string the sky with lace.
You who give to many an hour
The nurture of your silver shower
Have touched me with your tender grace.
Oh fleeting cloud, are you God's face?

The Fashion Show

A summer day is a procession of girls:
From green-gowned Morning, strewn with pearls,

To tawny Noon in garnet lace,
With gilded hair and gleaming face,

To see-through sleeves of Afternoon
Whose flowing mantles upward plume,

To Evening, dressed her very best
In turquoise skirts and purple vest,

With copper shawl around her swung,
Each tress of hair with roses hung,

Who runs her bath from a golden tap
And climbs into a gold tub's lap

Where silver water overflows,
Then, cleansed of color, off she goes

To indigo Night's attire,
And in the low glow of her fire,

Makes her way to bed and sleep
In velvet cushions, very deep.

Genesis

As the earth folds on itself, it seems to
Pound in beauty, and ardent rocks
Are fused and then cast away

And seas seize the rocks, making
Ground in beauty, and pummeled sands
Blare their granular array

And soils split for trees, which are
Crowned in beauty, their mobiles of jewels
Turning every which way

And buds, shyly closed, and tightly
Wound in beauty, spread apart their petticoats
To bare their display

And crickets sing the night, and Lunas
Gowned in beauty, and the Dark woos
The fireflies that bite it away

And I, walking by, am simply
Drowned in beauty, held hostage to a
Glory that takes my breath away

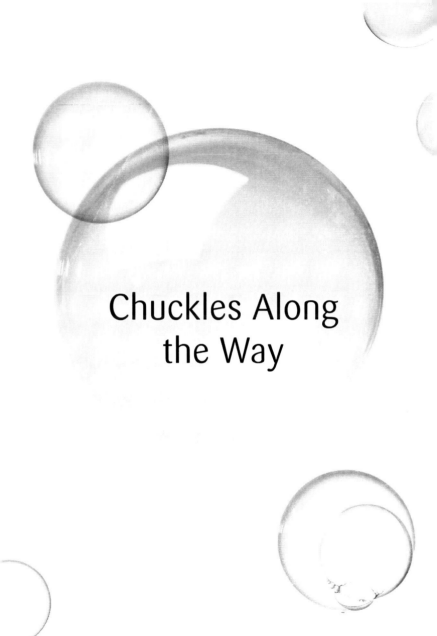

Chuckles Along
the Way

Yikes!

I brought the wrong glasses!
I brought the wrong map!
Did you ever show up
Feeling like that?

My mind is chewing itself again—
Just when I began to think it a friend.

Intensity

High or low, there's too much flow
That's how my feelings seem to go!

They launch me up! They slap me down!
Bounce back and forth from sky to ground!

A See-Saw am I—pound for pound,
Or worse—a yo-yo—round and round!

What's to serve me as a middle?
What's the answer to this riddle?

It's weird and weird and weird and weird—
Who's driving? Am I being steered?

Were extra gauges put in me
When I was still in factory?

Or were they just turned up so high
That always off the dial am I?

Please, Someone, turn down the sound
Slow the turntable whirling round

Please, Someone, put out the light
Every slide is much too bright

Change the focus, change the lens
Change my signal, make amends!

Shrink my feelings, make me numb
That I can hold to the middle some.

I need a surge protector, see?
A breaker for my circuitry

There's so much I stand to lose
Every time I blow a fuse.

Surfaces

Just when you get older
And start disliking yourself:
—Your limitations,
Your image in the mirror—

Your children start hating you, too,
Just to cheer you up.
And your husband might also,
Because of what your body is going through.

It must be alien to him;
It's alien to you.

It's the old heave-ho,
The rubbish heap for you
In biology's and the family's
And your own point of view.

Who set this up?
Can we sue?

I guess we must look underneath
The surfaces of things in order to renew.

Guess this is a new gestation in the series
Of gestations our souls grow through.

Don't resist it. Don't resist it at
all. Let it flow through.
There is always, every day forever,
A brand new you.

On Fire

Creaky Skeleton, how do I love thee?
Let me recite the ways!
With silver needles you thread me through,
Embroidering my days.

Creaky Skeleton, how do I love thee?
Let me recite the thrills!
The rosy flames in every joint
Compel me to swallow pills.

Creaky Skeleton, how I admire thee!
Thou tapestry of pain!
Aglow—Alight—with throbbing points,
Who resists thy reign?

Speechless am I in their rapturous clutch!
By thy charms continually slain!
Breathless, as it escalates too much!
Helpless in thy domain!

Thine exquisite art governs my heart
I tremble at every hour
Each anomalous hurt—oh! To be a young squirt!—
Pays homage to your power!

Captive am I, forevermore
In thy bond perverse
Until I locate the specialist
Who can all your wiles reverse!

Sad Sack Sacked

Failure is a sorry guy who comes on sorry feet
And sings you a sorry song, a song of defeat.

He really tries—and to his credit—
it's not his fault he's small,
But he can't stop you—it's pathetic—
and that's his big downfall.

So, you didn't get it right the first time you tried!
He thinks that will wipe you out,
and moves in, sounding snide.

Big deal! You'll try again! You've got reserves inside!
And as soon as you try again, he'll turn tail and hide!

For he's a bit of a coward, and has a fragile pride,
And almost no endurance, and
cannot strength abide.

You'll try again and again, however long it takes.
How on earth would people learn if
they didn't make mistakes?

There is no magic number—whatever he pretends—
And you are never under, if you're trying it again.

Mistakes are often your best friends:
they help and teach and guide,
And show you yet a little more, or flip a lens inside.

When no defeat can stop you,
it's quite a merry ride—
The ups and downs, the ins and outs,
the climb, and then the glide …

Poor Failure, he's a sorry case, he
skipped town, have you heard?
He left here without a trace when
he was *not* the last word.

Spanking Fun

Sometimes life is no spanking fun:
All that I do just gets undone!

I do the dishes; we use them again.
I wash the clothes; they stay clean when?

Lady Winter

If She ain't full of schemes and tropes
Like pock-marked moons and sugared slopes,
Then my name is Jack Robinson.

If this extended metaphor
Ain't anthropomorphism galore,
Then my name is Jack Robinson.

If imagery ain't freely flung and
Onomatopoeias frooply sprung,
Then my name is Jack Robinson.

If clots of curdled, creamy words
Don't conjure alliterative herds
Then my name is Jack Robinson.

If dazzling Snow Scene don't take kind
To folks who pay no never-mind
To beauty blinding as the sun,

Then, by the way, it's time you knew,
While we're discussing who is who,
My name ain't Jack Robinson.

Winter Limerick

Winter's in a sorry way;
Shaking his fist, though he may.
His prospects are bleaker
As he gets weaker,
Poor guy! He'll soon fade away.

Toe Holds in the Light

This Rich Crazy English

We sail *upwind* and downwind,
but at day's end *unwind*.
We love kith and *kin*, and to them would be *kind*.
A fish may have *fins*, just look and you'll *find*,
It's simply enough to boggle the mind!

This crazy English is delight and dismay!
However does one learn to spell its array?
Coincidence, evidence, or nonsense, you say?
And which would you rather, be prey, or just pray?

If you go to Hawaii, they give you a lei.
If you go to the beach, on the sand you may lay.
If horse-drawn through snow,
you will ride in a sleigh,
And if you go to work, you do it for pay.

If you're making bread, you knead up some dough.
If you're making salad, you slice tomato.
If you're playing Mozart, you might play oboe.
But this is all info you already know!

Oh seeds we may sow, and clothes we may sew,
A song on piano, we must play like so!
A song we may hear, as long as we're here,
Have nothing to fear, and are of good cheer!

The past tense of *throw*, we all know is *threw*,
But the past tense of *snow* is not ever *snew*.
Although the word *woe* spells like the word *shoe*
It is pronounced like *so* by me and by *you*.

We knead dough to bake and we need dough to buy;
On our faces and taters alike we have eyes;
Sometimes our moms make us raspberry pies,
And we all have occasions to which we must rise!

When things get too hum-drum,
we tend to be bored,
When we grow a garden, we might harvest gourds.
When we're under siege—overtaken by hordes—
They might find our riches, which
they're likely to hoard.

Ears of corn on our plates, on
our heads we have ears;
We have teeth in our mouths, we
have teeth in our gears;
We may tear out our hair, or burst into tears;
And we may have careers and still be in arrears!

How learn to read, and how learn to spell
A language like this? Little kids can tell
The ciphering horrors of lingo pell mell—
There's something unsettling,
and yet something swell

About the rich crazy English in which we can say
Wondrous things and their meanings convey!
Donkeys may bray, and horses may neigh,
Kids may be naughty, or they may obey—

But it's good to appreciate all we can say!
From quite long ago, right down to this day!
For our language can carry us up and away,
And our language can help us
with work and with play!

English is more than just what you are hearing;
The spelling keeps changing;
I wonder who's steering?
Molded by history—with much interfering—
And isn't it lovely, and utterly endearing?

A Question

When it comes to vacuuming,
My son spends five minutes
On any job that takes me
Over thirty.
He covers yards while
I crawl through inches.

Yet when we're finished,
The results look much
The same.
So what am I vacuuming
Out of the rug?
Self-blame?

Ode to an Outhouse
at an Old Farm Sale

I've been at this estate all day;
I've heard the auctioneer
Offer up each thing for sale, his voice fresh in my ear.
I've walked and looked, I've sat and
looked, I've napped within my car;
I started a book, finished the book,
and yet, still here I are!

I've stood on one foot and the other, edgy as can be,
Tried every ploy I can to avoid necessity.
But I guess I'll have to face it, at least eventually,
I'll have to make the dreaded
trip to the outdoor privy.

Ah, a trip to the outhouse can be
a mighty fitting thing!
I don't need to mention the relief that it can bring.
But the flies that buzz around me
had best not bite or sting!
It's music to my ears, when they are on the wing.

For sitting in this welcome, private, sweet amenity
When the insects go to silence it
can mess with your serenity
Where are the pesky creatures, you
sit and have to wonder;
Have they found a patch of skin
behind, or worse, down under?

"Oh please, let this job be fast!"
you pray the outhouse gods
And you meditate and ponder
what really are the odds,
And you try to deal with sitting
there; it really is a bore!
And you try to deal with guilt when
others rattle at the door!

Christine Van Brunt   82

Yes, I doubt the *literati* have the slightest notion
Of the study one could make of
the full range of emotion
Which Everyman experiences in this lowly edifice
From anxiety to boredom to guilt and then—to bliss!

I thank you, lowly outhouse! A refuge, Thou for me!
For there are times throughout the
day one welcomes privacy!
I'm feeling so much better than I did before.
I leave you now with thanks and
praise … and … ever so much more!

Civilization and Its Discontents

Inside us all, lethargic lions,
—Sedate, dignified—
Bask in the sun,

Having forgotten that certain soaring
That comes with roaring.
(It is verboten.)

And such is our kingdom,
And such is our boredom,
We don't even know
We've forgotten.

My Humanity
and Yours

Fundamentals

Huge would be the cataclysm
In any worldview's catechism
If our tenets we tried to tell
Without the stuff inside our cells.

However differing our theologies,
Premises or ideologies,
Greater yet would be the chasm
If we were lacking protoplasm.

Agree, then, there'd be hell to pay
If we were lacking DNA,
And arguments just couldn't start
Without our intracellular art.

If thanks is part of your worldview,
Then heed your cells, and thank them too!
Mind your physiology;
Offer praise, without apology.

True Grit

Stuff happens.
Facts are.
On the best of walks
Shoes pick up rocks.

Gnats get in your eyes
On gorgeous summer days
Interesting, isn't it, how grit
Accompanies the most beautiful of gifts?

Real people everywhere
—In homes, in jobs, in politics—
All grate together: rocks in a tumbler.
Do we all come out polished? I wonder.

Ever Think

Ever think about how much
Feeling is felt that is left unsaid?
That couldn't be said?

Like the way you feel
When your beloved comes into the room?

Like the way you feel
When your beloved comes home?

Like the way you feel
When he sits in his chair,

And you know—your cells know—he is there.
He is there.

Blinders

The *ground* we stand on and *gravity*
Are so constantly with us, in our company,
We consider them not, separately,
As anything really that we should see.
We just assume they're forever and free.

And so with the persons we love best:
We bask in their presence, know their caress,
Lounge in their love; with them, know rest;
Sometimes, so close, we mistake them for us!
Fail to see or thank them, assume too much.

Our Inner Deep

Inside us, our own inner deep
Has currents and turbulence,
Power and calm,
Little eddies, big tides,
Quiet tidal pools, teeming with life—

Of all these things
We are comprised.

On the topside, a cradling lap
Of gentle rocking
Can become a towering force
Of breakers bashing,
And then a heaving bosom
Of unending peace.

This is our mixed
And rich experience.

In whatever its state, the salt and
Swell of this ever-moving deep is
Always alive, always filled with power,
Volume, movement, grace, incredible
Force, and—oh—so much space!

Such faces and moods
We harbor and brood!

How is it the same watery terrain
That can rock and ease
And show barely a crease
Can then thrash and kill,
Become jagged with peaks
And then return to a seamless peace?

And how do we navigate these waters—
We who are their sons and daughters?

Doubting Thomas

Doubting Thomas is my best friend;
He clings until the bitter end.
Just when I think I've dealt with pride,
Both the flop and the flip side,
Here Thomas is right by my side.

"Are you *really* made for joy?" he'll ask
"Think this productive streak will *last*?"
It was only yesterday
I told Thomas to go away
And he went; I saw him go, but hey—

He knows my weak spots, every one,
Pokes and provokes them just for fun:
"Do you think you're *good enough*?"
"You'll be *too weak* when the going's tough!"
"What makes you think *you've* got the stuff?"

I send him off. I do, and then,
He's back—and I invite him in!
"Are you really *worth* all this?"
"Don't you have to *be special* to feel bliss?"
"Aren't *they* much better than *you* at this?"

I've known him as long as I've known myself
He's the shadow on my higher self.
He's persistent; I'll give him that.
And I know he'll keep coming back,
But I have something that he lacks.

I have the Truth, while he has lies,
And though he tries and tries and tries,
He won't stop me anymore,
May he come right in the door.
I'm wiser than I was before.

And even if in error perverse
With him I actually converse,
I mend my ways, and pretty quick.
I see him for what makes him tick.
I pity him, for he is sick.

Longing

Find me with your searchlight eye,
Scrutinize and magnify,
Risk your soul to other sea,
Learn my secret majesty.

Comb my waves with nets of light;
Understand their molten might:
Faceted and changing moods—
Pewter, silver, sapphire goods.

Comprehend me, sound my depths;
Measure hidden monoliths.
Sweep the caverns of my mind;
Sift the silt and treasures find:

Wonders from remotest lands,
Filigree and golden bands.
Turn them over in your hands;
Take them with you, all you can.

Weigh my ingots, count my crowns;
Gather all and take them home.
Mine my trophies, every one.
Save me from oblivion.

The Challenge

Wonderful is the one who can hold me
Without holding me in,
Who can enfold me in such a way I am
Free to expand.

It takes a vessel strange
—Elastic, large, and living—
It takes a heart with range
—Giving and forgiving—

It takes deep, undaunted scope
To weather my altitudes!
As Walt Whitman said,
I am large. I contain multitudes.

Questions

The punctuality of the stars
The precision of the flowers
Man can measure, count, and quantify.

But what methods or schemes
Can man possibly contrive
To plumb an aching lover's sigh?

And what calculations, I wonder,
Can sum the salt oceans
In an aching lover's eye?

Pretty People

Pretty people pay a price
For being pretty.
Other people won't play nice,
Assuming pretty
People already get enough
Of the stuff
Everybody wants, everybody needs,
And that there is a scarcity
Of it:

Attention, love, visibility, notice,
Validation, acceptance, the
Whole
Bottomless
List

Which translates into
These underlying needs:
—Saving Face
—Contributing
—Belonging

That universal prayer
We don't know we pray
Everyday.

All are codes for even
Deeper needs:
—To be valued
—To have worth

A drive to push through
Obscurity to the light of day,
To unfold and live bold,
Show our own bright face,
Shed our own perfumed
Petals on the visible
Common ground,

Be an "I am"
Be found

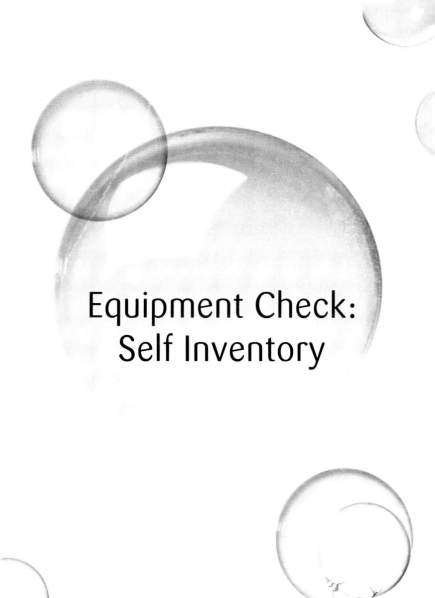

Equipment Check: Self Inventory

Love Song to My Tutors

I wanted to be the honesty of the rock
Squat, solid, heavy, hard
Inflexible, lasting
Unapologetically cold unless warmed by sun or fire;
I wanted to be that unequivocal.

I wanted to be the self-disclosure of the flower
Wand-like, weightless, soft, silken
Pliant, fleeting
Shooting up blue flumes,
Sending missives of perfume;
I wanted to be that true to my tune.

I wanted to be the self-propulsion of the water
That ceaseless weave of liquid light
Pure transparent might, pealing and reeling,
Pushing everything along, mocking obstacles,
Flinging songs;
I wanted to be that unswerving of purpose.

And then I came to find
I had to be me, that being Human
Was my honesty,
Owning and honing what
Is best in me—my own little spark
Of Divinity—

But oh, these others—
The rock, the flower, the water—
They tutor me.

So, Who Am I Anyway?

Sometimes I'm a Hero with a cheer that never tires.
The *Right* and the *Good* are my best-tended fires.
I have a boundless joy, and strength that multiplies;
The more I give, the more I get,
in unending supplies.

Then *that voice* in my head tells me I am really fine,
And no one else compares, and aren't I just divine?

Sometimes I'm a Judge, with a long and doleful face,
Sifting souls for fitness, souls for disgrace,
Obsessed with people's differences,
a coward on the run,
See a new act to admire—get totally undone.

Then *that voice* in my head judges me harshest of all
Whatever I dished out, and more,
comes doubling back to call.

Sometimes I'm a Junkie, seeking center stage.
My un-sated craving is the stuff of *every* page.
I want all the attention, and hoard up all the love,
Sucking all my sources dry, and always on the move.

The more I work for notice, the less the notice comes
And *that voice* in my head says I'll never be the one.

Hero, Judge, and Junkie: each face feels so alone
One holds itself aloft in such a higher tone;
One traverses byways, pressing blood from stone;
One thirsts for approval; it has none of its own.

If I could but love myself! Then I could love us all!
But of all the orders in this world—
that one is most tall.

Putting the Pieces Together

So meet each other, people! You are a special trinity:
Faces of the self-same soul: faces all of me!
Hero, please meet Junkie; and
Junkie please meet Judge!
You each could help the other, and
not your strengths begrudge.
Now won't you work together, and
start right here with me?
Give me self-acceptance with your special synergy?

Hero, you are *Ethos*, my credibility,
Good will, scruples, principles, and fair integrity.
Junkie, you are *Pathos*, not just all need, but heart.
You are the seat of empathy and
where emotions start.
Judge, you are *Logos*, meant to evaluate
The facts of the matter, the logic, status, state.

All three are required the whole soul to guide.
Each need inform the other to
human health provide.
It's when they're separated the soul feels so denied.
As much as two are "cut off," the
third's too big and wide,
Taking over and skewing one's full humanity.
Instead of heart and mind and
will, you have an amputee.

So Hero, bring your energy, and
the seeds of joy it sows;
Junkie, bring the need for love
that sets your heart aglow;
Judge, bring your searchlight—
that sight without repose.
Hold hands all, and circle 'round,
toes aligned with toes!
Then I can put behind me the cause of all my woes,
Any *severed piece of self* that would as *whole self* pose.

With Hero's Will and Judge's Mind,
and Junkie's Heart, you see
You three can help me find a better path to being me.
Show some daring: stop comparing,
except myself to me.
Show some caring: start preparing
me to welcome me.
Make me your special project; let others all go free!
And the best I have will rise up,
and a giant well-spring be!

Tussles with
Technology

Inner Resources

The TV went out,
Wouldn't you know,
In the middle of my favorite show

I tried all the buttons
On the dumb remote
But couldn't get the stupid thing unchoked

I whined and cursed,
Got a bit abusive,
And my ugliness waxed more effusive

Then…

I took a deep breath,
Stilled myself,
And to make the best of it, I willed myself

I lit a candle,
Sang a song,
Went and put the kettle on

Washed the dishes
Steeped some tea,
Thought how life is good to me

Played piano
Sang a prayer
Thanked God for music everywhere

Heard the silence
Heard the clock
Heard the breath in my body talk

Made friends with Quiet
Greeted Peace
Breathed in Sweet Life, and met Release

And you know,
When that TV wouldn't start,
I think I got the better part

Outpaced

In this sleek world of
Molded plastic tops for Styrofoam cups
In this accelerated realm of
Cell phones that stay relevant for maybe five months

In this sprinting sphere where
Obsolescence outruns the learning curve
And trickier, slicker models of everything
Overturn the market

Where the duration of knowledge
Has the thickness of cellophane
And the new cellophane
Has more hold

Would that my brain
Could so mold to all the newness
With the same
Transparent grace

Technology

Things that technology is very good at:

Speed
Communication
Thermometers
Telephones
Illustrations
Photography
Acceleration
Convenience
Obsolescence
Efficiency
Multi-tasking

Things that technology isn't so good at:

Quality
Communication
Thermometers
Telephones

Illustrations
Customer Service
Bedside Manner
Cartoons
Neighborliness
Being
Spending Time

Things that technology doesn't do at all:

Listening—to the creak of the porch swing,
The wind in the birches,
The rain on the panes,
The hope in the words

Hearing—the unsaid things:
The infirmity in a person's walk,
The clock ticking,
The illness in a person's talk

Top-of-the-Line
Friend Software

You might want to shop,
If you dare,
For these top-of-the-line versions
Of Friend software:

Attentive Listener
Easy Listener with Acceptance Settings
Deep Listener
Live Listener
Top to Bottom Listener
Listener for as Long as it Takes
Listener Who Doesn't Fix It
Listening As The Best Fix-It
Encourager with Advanced *Where You Are* Settings
Feedback Filter with *Multiple Sensitivity* Settings
Practical Tips Suggester with
All Due Respect Settings
Uber Belly Laughs Inducer

Uber Perspective Dispenser with
Enhanced Sensitivity Settings
Self Validation Remediator
Self Validation Progenitor
Hearts of Calm
Courageous Listener with *High Risk Tolerance*
Settings and Multiple *Climbs Into Your Head* Settings
Radical Doubt Reducer with
Worry Stomper Adaptor
Worry Stomper
Condensed Milk of Wisdom
Useless Story Slayer
Drama Detox and Dialysis
Challenger
Customizable Challenger
Consciousness Stretcher
Consciousness Stretcher with Expansion Extender

The last one, which includes all prior upgrades
Is very difficult to find.
To pursue it, look online for the name
Friend Software 8.9.

Try Writing Software Requirements for These

It is ridiculous
The volume and variation
Of beauty packed into any one thing,
And overflowing out of one anything

The dappling light on a leaf—
The fleeting light show on clouds—

To catalog it—
To list it all out—
To capture all its changes—
Moment to moment

Would take all the space on earth
And the rest of your life.

Christine Van Brunt

Arrested by Peace

Hey, Bella

Hey, Bella, Beautiful One—
Uncoil your beautiful face

I hold your face in my two hands
Your loveliness in my two hands

Give me this moment, Bella,
And just let me gaze

I love—I love—
Your beautiful face.

Be still, my Beautiful One.
Let me hold you

Here, here, let me hold
And enfold you

That we keep the moment
Let us quiet the race

And breathe, breathe,
Breathe, breathe

And slow down, yes,
Slow down the pace.

Feel our two breaths,
Expanding, contracting

Wave after wave after wave
Transacting

Thanks for nestling
With me here

I love so much
When you are near.

My thumbs trace your brows
Touch your lidded eyes

You are smiling—now
If you could see your face!

And your smile is so
Like a rosy sunrise

With your glowing skin
And the light in your eyes

You are smiling—even
As your brows I trace

Bella, Bella, Bella—
Luminous grace

Fresh as the dew
Oh the countenance of you!

Give me this moment, Bella,
And just let me gaze

I love—I love—
Your beautiful face.

Welcome Stillness

Beloved Silence, my next of kin
Big as the booming air
When did you manage to climb in my skin?
How long have you been here?

Gifts of Old

Old trees,
Old dogs,
Old men—

Weighty things,
Rooted things—
Slip a welcome stillness into one's consciousness.

In their very quiet, they sing
Of a contentment that undergirds everything.

In their presence, one is at home:
Old trees whisper like the kettle on the stove;
Old dogs breathe like the fire in the hearth;
Old men doze and nap
In the spirit of a vast and timeless lap—

Soothing the unquiet mien,
Slowing the hopping nerve and vein—

Dispensing
Comfort like a soft
Murmuring rain.

Old trees,
Solid and gray
Stand and stay ...

Old dogs
Lie on their sides,
Breathe and sigh ...

Old men,
Whiskers on chin,
Look on and grin ...

Christine Van Brunt

Perfect Moment

Thanks be to all the moments of my life
For bringing me to this now,
To this perfect moment.

Beloved Silence, Here You Are Again

Oh Beloved Silence, deep in my favorite chair,
I love how it is that in quiet, you are so loudly there.

White Space

For me,
White Space
Is that quiet place

Where Creation
Moves ...

Calls up a new
Face, a new

Species, perhaps a new
Race.

A land of thrall.
An open clearing
That is the origin
Of all.

A lovely,
Clean and linen land
Of fresh snowfalls,
Deep snows,
Where anything that moves
Is seen as it comes
And goes.
And if it comes at night,
Can be tracked
By footfall.

I love setting a
New Creation
Down
Onto this canvas,
Lovingly, gently.

Is it beautiful?
Will it run?
I never know.

Christine Van Brunt 132

I never know
Until I see it go,
Watch it trace
Its shadow
Across the snow.

Toe Holds in the Light

Quips for Power Trippers

In the Name of Love

When "I love you" means:
"You have to be just like I want you to be"
Something else is really going on.

Even if the person saying it doesn't realize—
That highly qualified and stacked-against-you
"I love you" might just be a lie—

The lie of an ill person, struggling—
In the self-esteem area—
To get by.

It's a Code for "I need you to be a certain way,
So I can feel better about myself.
To fix me."

That is not the same thing as love.
That is a problem with self-love.

And it is a bottomless pit
Because the cure they seek
Is not the cure for it.

For they have mistakenly placed
The cure in you.
It is neither your responsibility
Nor in your power to do.

There is no cure, without the person's
Permission. Unless he himself wills it,
Gets help for it, and does the work.

So when the person says those words
To manipulate you,
Be aware so you can see through—

And don't be harmed or taken in;
Keep yourself safe
In your own inner space.

Listen for love that is true.
And you can have that,
Starting with you.

Caregivers, Caution!

Fragile flowers die daily,
Half-bloomed,
Because they are called
By name too soon,
When they might be
Quite a different bloom.

Whoever, by insisting, can call up
Tulips any sooner?
Whoever, by shaming, can unlock
Lilacs any more fragrant?
Whoever, by naming, can transform
Pansies into peonies?

Be patient,
Ye who would love flowers;
Put in the hours.

You must wait and see
What wondrous blooms
They come to be.

To appreciate means
Not only *see*, but also *wait*.

Give lots of room.
Each, in its own time,
Comes into season
Late or soon,
Uncurling and unfurling
A lifelong, lingering bloom.

The flowers we're talking about
Are *people*, the little people
In your care, so take heed:

Beware lest *your* notion
Of the flower
Becomes a
Vase you
Stick it in
That by and by
Becomes its tomb.

Safe Deposit

I rent a safe deposit box;
The cost is nothing compared to the savings.

What is in the box
Is the only thing between me and starvation.

I keep my voice in the box.
It needs to be in a locked vault. Hidden. Safe.

Before I had the box, I got mugged a lot.
I got mugged so many times
I was afraid to walk down the street
Or sit at the kitchen table and try to eat.

I was afraid of what I might speak
Or think or dream or want or wonder.
My skull had suffered so much thunder
—With or without a lightning warning.

I shied from shadows and from light.
My night was day; my day was night.
I shuddered at the sound of my own voice.

So I took my voice, my honest, true voice,
And rented me a safe deposit box,
And there I keep it
Where no one will ever find it
Unless I say so.

Gives me a kind of safety, you know?
From criticisms and condemnations.

I've been robbed so many times
I'm afraid to own anything.

I tried to throw my voice away;
But it sticks to me and sticks out of me,
And will always have its say.
So I have hidden it away
Not to abandon, but to safeguard.
I go to visit it sometimes
When the vault is open.
I make an appointment.

The rest of the time, if I need to,
I go around wooden-headed
And empty-handed,
So much less afraid
Because my voice isn't with me.

We keep apart, me and my art.
If we're caught together—!

Only this prayer have I.

Dear Mr. Vault,
Whose many spacious rooms hold so many dreams
And give none of them away,

Please stay open so I can make appointments.

It's all I have, don't you see,
Between me and starvation.

Power Imbalance

Who is this little god
Who has such mighty power?
When she rails, what happens?
Does all the milk turn sour?

Does the sun fall from the sky
So no one knows the hour?
Who is this little god
Who has such mighty power?

Is her moral outrage
Really any louder
Than the flood of Noah
With its rising water?

Does she really have such force
—Or does she merely wish it?
I say, call her bluff!
What happens when *you* dish it?

Is she god almighty?
Shall we bang the tom-tom drum?
Or is she simply mortal woman
Having a tantrum?

Don't let her take your crops;
Stop the rites and sacrifices;
Don't let her eat your beating heart;
You have better choices!

If you must serve a god so caustic,
It might be time to turn agnostic.

Yearning for Expansion

Define me—
That I'll be—

Frozen

in your prison.

But watch and see
When the ice goes out
How I'll sing
And how I'll shout—

The

Power

of *that* hour!

Compost for
the Soul

Good

This, this moment,
I am doing exactly what I should be doing,
And it is good.

This, this moment,
You are doing exactly what you should be doing,
And it is good.

Empowered

Not a little chick am I anymore,
No longer newly hatched,
Nor so wet, barely fluffed out yet,
Nor scarcely unlocked.

Not scared, anymore, as I once was,
To open up my voice,
To take to the air, to rise in flight
To run around the block.

Now, I stand, a Phoenix gold,
Glinting in the sun,
Eyeing heaven, loving light,
Raising my brow at hawks.

Flowering

Hello, you

Are you in bloom?
I thought I knew from your perfume!
I am too!

Herald me.
Sniff *my* perfume!
I am bursting with each bloom!
And *so happy!*

Can you tell by my perfume
That I am bloomed
And happy be?
Herald me!

Ode to Respect and Care

You were the first
To handle these leaves
Of my unshown self.

These fine filaments
Of soul, you were the first
To turn over in your hands.

Their tender tracery
You viewed still when
They were new,

And this shy architecture
You knew before
It barely grew.

This voiced fragrance
You sniffed reverently,
Then left intact upon the tree.

These succulent blooms
You never assumed
Were yours to take

As your very own
—To carry away and
Arrange just so—

To grace a vase
In a room alone.
You saw, you

Respected, then you left them
To sway free. You saw
They were mine.

You left them for me.

Soft Power

A Woman is like
Water,

Her fingers of light
Erasing dams,
Moving pebbles,
Sculpting stone.

Her dancing curls and
Wrinkling folds, ever
Press their silver swirls
Into the bedrock which
Clasps them—
Twirling tunnels,
Smoothing jagged places down,
Bringing to light all the layers,
Making all sharp edges round.

A Woman is like
Water,

She can shape and
Reshape the solid immovable,
Cutting new channels.
She can be held
—Molded and molding—
Slow-dance tight,
Bumping up new features
—Stark and fantastic—
And bring them to light.
Her flowing currents chisel
Gorges, and hold up to the sun
Proportions of canyons
—Becoming and become.

A Woman is like
Water,

Her voice is a chorus of bells,
Now high and tremulous,
Now low and gurgling, or
Soft, hushing
Bubble whisper.
She can sweep or suck away
Stuck things in swishing spray.

She can toll and loll in a
Consoling way,
Or play—rocking and licking—
Or flay—roiling and ripping—
Calling powerfully
All to the fray.

A Woman is like
Water,

Her tumult of pearls is a
Bubbling commotion of
Chase and flight;
Her weaving light is
A tumbling cycling of
Falls and rills.
She makes a
Communion of drops
—Each in itself a
Separate world,
A full spectrum,
A single twinkling cell—
Altogether merging, melding
Coalescing as one
Into a seamless
River run.

A Woman is like
Water,

Musically flowing
Holding and harboring Life,
Uncontainable,
Shape shifting,
Now in a torrent
Of white water and foam
a sprite,
Now a barely moving
Bottomless pool
Where trout hide.

Losses,
Expectations

Amputation

There's a gut-lived belief
That people who are Larger than Life
Are larger than death too. They're not.

The body's belief
Is they're just out for a spell,
But they're coming back. They don't.

The problem becomes
There's a hole here now
That nothing else plugs. What could?

So there's a hole in your heart
That tugs at your life,
And it doesn't let up. So you cry.

And that upsets people
Who talk among themselves,
"She's not taking it well," and they try

To get away after saying
Something trite like
"Time will heal." Oh, really?

You try to believe them, you think
It will stop; with time,
You won't remember.

It doesn't, and you do.

And with others you can tell
It's getting to the point
Where they won't put up

With the discomfort they feel
Because you're so sad,
So they blame you.

So (even when they don't ask) you lie.

And you feel angry and betrayed that
You should have to hide—as though shameful—
The feelings you feel, yet you buy

Into it enough to ask why it hurts so much
Why don't I just let it go?
Why does it matter so much?

Here's why:

Because that loved person's being here, and that
Loved person's not being here
Makes—made—makes

A *vast* difference.

Permission

You don't need permission to grieve.

Just because people are uncomfortable,
They think you should stop
So *they* can feel better.

Do your honest grieving.
Do it for as long as it takes for as long as you need
Until you're done.

The time will come—especially if you don't rush it—
When you will be ready to make peace
And move on.

Severed

Dad pulled me through the sky
—The sky was our connection—
It tugged me to him always, like a fish on the line.

Together or apart,
The sky caused us reflection.
I'd think of him when I saw it, every single time.

He's gone now, my Dad.
Now I shun that direction.
I can't, don't, won't—even look at the sky.

For My Dad: Cooking Fire

In the western sky, see the cooking fire
Where the gods' supper is simmering,
And tending it, the goddesses,
Their robes around them shimmering?

Watch ho! How the chieftain gods
From the Four Winds assemble!
Their molten steeds streak the sky;
Its golden canyons tremble!

After supper, the mighty ones
—As the fire slowly dies—
Keep their council quietly,
And the coals shine in their eyes.

Christine Van Brunt

Meal Remembered

An irregular yolk of a frying egg
Is tonight's setting sun,
Its gold orb is rimmed round by a foaming froth
Like a floating island.

Popping egg whites—in too hot a pan—
Are the surrounding clouds,
Pocked and puckered with raggedy edges,
And the cooking is loud.

A sputtering pan is the whole changing sky
On this particular night,
And the only camera is just my eye,
And, oh, what a sight.

Social Justice:
The Deep End

Little Lamb

You are visible to me,
My little lamb, my little lamb,
You who yearns to set them free,
You who yearns to set them free,
You're visible to me

How you listen when you pray,
My little lamb, my little lamb,
Soaking in that living ray,
Soaking in that living ray,
Light splashes when you pray

Your heart
Is an open door
Where the living waters pour
Where the living waters pour
And the water
It is warm

Oh, Ye Dear People,
Come and swim,
Healing waits for you within
Healing waits for you within,
Come in
From the storm

They are with you evermore,
My little lamb, my little lamb,
Folded to your inner core
Folded to your inner core
They're with you evermore

In the park you see a man,
My little lamb, my little lamb,
Shivering in a blanket thin
Shivering in a blanket thin
You go back to take him in

And there you find four more

Oh
The ocean roars
Breaking through your every pore
Breaking through your every pore
'Til you are sick and sore

Oh
Your blood; it roars
You'd offer a homeless world your floor,
You'd offer a homeless world your floor
Aching to do more

The world cries out
With all
Its need
Your hearing heart, it hears and hears
Your hearing heart, it hears and hears
And bleeds

In the Fold

As the mother that I am
My little lamb, my little lamb
I imagine the Shepherd's dad
I imagine the Shepherd's dad
Laying on his healing hand

Saying, Come to me, my precious lamb,
I who am the Great I Am
I who am the Great I Am
Would your heart relieve …

Come and sleep my little lamb
I who am the Great I Am
I who am the Great I Am
Call you not to grieve …

Come and let me fold you in
Deep in rest, I'll hold you in
You can go out there again
Your friendly hand extend again
And all the crying heed

Shutting out that awful din
My little lamb, my little lamb
Just right now I'll hold you in,
And when we sally forth again
I will take the lead ...

Rest now from that wild ride
My little lamb, my little lamb
For yet awhile, may ye bide,
Yet awhile may ye bide,
And on my waters feed ...

Little Subservient
Me

Exhausted People Pleaser

Always I am swimming this ocean,
This ocean without any shore—
Tossed and wrung out in its dark, creasing motion,
Flayed by its force and its roar!

Oh, I am weary, and the water is deep,
And the watery mountains have sides that are steep;
I gasp for an island of sweet-breathing sleep,
Where striving can cease evermore,
Where striving can cease evermore.

Sometimes I feel I am gaining;
Sometimes I imagine a shore!
If I add to the muscle, add to the straining,
I might cover more than before!

But I am weary, and the water is deep;
The watery mountains have sides that are steep;
I doubt that an island will offer its keep,
Where striving could cease evermore,
Where striving could cease evermore.

If I push air through lungs that are aching
—If my burning chest I ignore—
If I push blood through veins that are breaking,
Might I then find rest on some shore?

For I am weary and the water is deep;
The watery mountains have sides that are steep;
I'm sliding backwards and slipping beneath,
And I can't go on any more.
I can't go on any more.

Spineless

Silly Putty is my name;
I am a twisty doll!
When I start feeling really big,
I'm shriveled down to small!

One person tells me one thing;
Another tells me else
An arbiter is wanting!
Not pleasing *all* just smells!

Over any shape just drop me
And to it I'll conform!
Press me against any printed thing
And I'll wear it as my own!

Do mermaids fly trapezes?
Do airplanes go by rails?
If you told me so, I might believe
That birthday cakes had tails!

I need an Alka-Seltzer!
I need a Bufferin!
I'm kneaded, but hardly rising,
I live scrunched up in my can.

Spent Game

Weeping instead of sleeping
What is the game we run?
What is it that was done?
That now should be undone?

The game of people pleasing
I won with as a child
Is not a winning game now.
No one is beguiled.

Excepting me; I still am—
Using it as a guide—
Though it brings me only shame
Where once it brought me pride.

Every time I pull it out,
People condescend,
Isn't she cute—not quite grown up—
Look at her pretend.

Then I see myself as they do,
And I almost choke on sick!
The seeds I sow grow opposites
Of the crop I want to pick!

It's the only game in town!
It's the only game I know!
Until I find a substitute,
How do I let it go?

Christine Van Brunt   184

You Too

You think joy is for other people, and not for you.
Don't you believe it; it's not true.
This is an abundant universe. There's room
For you aboard the joy train too.

You fear your success would rob other people.
It won't. Real successes never do.
Set your intention right now to produce value—
And you'll raise everybody else's status too.

This is an abundant universe. The model
Of scarcity is an erroneous view.
Just another one of the lies of
—You Know Who.

The universe is behind you all the way.
You don't have to stop, stay blocked,
Toss or lock your gifts away.

The world is waiting for them. But we are patient.
You will know when you are ready to own them
And state them. On that day…

You will say, "These are the desires of my heart!"
Come what may. "Come out, come out!
Shine, shine, shine
in the light of day!"

Self-Talk or
Self-Toxic

Conversation

Some say you shouldn't talk to yourself.
But here's a question. Is there any human being
More important in your life

You could be talking to?
I suggest that whether you talk
out loud to yourself or not,
You're actually always holding a conversation.

When does that cloying voice in your head ever cease
Its steady stream of stuff, either eating
away at you on the inside
Or buffering and building you up?

How is that conversation going? Is it fair? Is it kind?
Is it good? Is it as respectful of you as you would
Be to a best friend?

If no, then you'd better be saying it out loud,
So you can hear yourself.
And put the bully beating up on you out.

Because the voice in your head is not
Necessarily you. And, if it's ripping on you
It's not likely true, and should be
subject to peer review.

Start with You

When you think thoughts of love,
Start with you.
When you speak words of love,
Start with you.

When you act out of love,
When you're gentle as a dove,
When you speak the truth in love,
Start with you.

Know the purpose of love,
First, is you.
So steep yourself in love,
Yes, do.

Pour it out, drink it up,
Overflow every cup,
And at Love's table sup,
Start with you.

Sweet and Good

You are sweet and good.
Replace you, nothing could.
Way down deep in the who of you
Is the ever-evolving stew of you
And you are sweet and good.

You are sweet and good.
Forget that word called "should."
In the inter-connecting glue of you
Is the ever-distilling You of you
You are sweet and good.

You are sweet and good.
Improve you nothing could.
Every day adds the new of you
To the blood and bone and true of you
And you are sweet and good.

Christine Van Brunt

192

Voice of Discouragement

I was feeling down and lonely;
I was feeling down and sad;
I was feeling life was lousy;
So I started doing bad.

It made me mad that life was so,
No matter what I planned,
My dreams would melt away like snow,
And empty leave my hand.

I decided Life was a liar!
I decided Time was a tease!
I decided Work was wasted!
Might as well do as I please!

What difference do your choices make
When you have no control?
What difference is the path you take?
You cannot make the goal.

When failure is a way of life,
And you *never* measure up,
You hate yourself and grieve the life
That might as well be up,

And you cry yourself to sleep at night,
And you cry when you wake up …
Then what is left to do?
What is left of you?

Wisdom of a Child: What Ethan Wrote in Fifth Grade

I am a painting
Of a clarinet.
Air is rushing out of me
As soon as it comes in.
My background is green, but
Sometimes, in the glare, it is red.
My reed breaks sometimes,
But it is always replaced.
People look at me, and think
I am a bad painting.
But in my painter's eyes
I am a masterpiece.

There is So Much More to You

There is so much more to you
Than the sum of all your thoughts
There is so much more to you
Than all your pans and pots
Than all your pictures on the wall
All your beds and cots
All the books lining your hall
All the mantels for your clocks
All the cars in your garage
Designer jeans, designer socks.

There is so much more to you
Than the emotions on your sleeve
Or in your heart and in your hopes
Buried underneath
There is so much more to you
Than the things that pitch and heave
Like fear and doubt and guilt about

What you did, did not achieve
Than all your choices, behaviors,
Preferences, and peeves.

There is so much more to you
Than your title where you work
Or the function you perform
From the cleaner to the clerk
To the head honcho who gets
The best parking and the perks
Whether you genuinely smile
Or really only smirk
There is so much more to you
Than who you are at work

There is so much more to you
Than whatever meets the eye
Whether your eyes are brightest green
Your cheekbones nice and high
How thin or wide or tall or small
Whether you laugh or cry
Whether your hair is long or short
Curly, straight, or fried
There is so much more to you
Than whatever meets the eye.

There is so much more to you
Than the voice that's in your head
Churning out its endless lists
Of what you want or dread
Or things you ought to do today
Or someday before you're dead
And also those things you don't dare
Do lest you get criticized
Also the things you'd only do
If guaranteed a prize.

There is so much more to you
Than your clever, cunning mind
There is so much more to you:
That Consciousness behind—
All the on-the-surface stuff
All the events in time
All the traffic in your thoughts
All stories that confine
All titles, roles, and masks
All memorized lines—

It's that Connection to your Higher Self
—And to all that is sublime—
Which longs to wake within you
—The fullness waiting in you—
To shine its light all through you,
To vibrate and renew you
And longs to warm and tend you
To fill and free and mend you
And love and call and send you,
And billow and extend you,
—And you may claim it at any time.

Hazards of Self-Talk

Sometimes it's astonishing how
we speak to ourselves!
Under cover of privacy,
We say things we would never say to someone else.
Mean things. Hurtful things.

Observe yourself. Catch yourself. Teach yourself
To treat yourself at least
As well as you treat other people. Pretend you are
Speaking aloud to someone else
In front of witnesses.

Conservation of Worth

Who are you when you're brought up short
And Adversity brings a bad report?
What attitude do you choose every day
Regardless of whether things go your way?

How is it for you when you're down and out,
And the world makes clear it's not you it's about?
How fares your character, its wealth and health?
How is it that you treat yourself?

As an honored guest in your soul's own home?
Or cast abroad to roam alone?
What stalks your mind? What hides in stealth?
What's your self-talk? What say you to yourself?

I accept myself … I bless myself … ?
I tried my best … with all the strength I possessed?
It's okay … I'll try again … ?
What matters is I try, not that I win?

Good for you, if you steep all day
In the encouraging words to yourself you say.
And succumb not to self-loathing lies
Designed to rob you of the prize

Of a joyful life, full of mirth
Overflowing with sense of worth,
Perfect, whole, and ever new,
Where your most trusted friend is you.

Stuck or Free

Rudderless

Rudderless my ship, on an angry sea,
Always shipping water, drowning silently.
Blown by every wind, driven to her knees,
Sometimes stuck in the shallows,
wishing for a breeze.
Where was the Captain?
Dreaming dreams that she could be
On a different ship, on a different sea ...

But you're my Anchorman! Hold me steady,
Steady as she goes, steady while she blows.
And I'll not fear the wind; I stand ready,
Ready with each roll, ready with my soul
To learn the ropes.

When there came a gale, the Captain couldn't win!
Always sailed full sail—didn't know to take them in!
Such was her belief, the vessel she was in
Somehow caused all the grief and conjured the wind!
And so the Captain, out of need, came to plead
From her prison ship to be freed ...

But you're my Anchorman! Hold me steady,
Steady as she goes, steady while she blows.
And I'll not fear the wind; I stand ready,
Ready with each roll, ready with my soul
To learn the ropes.

When her decks were drenched,
submerged rocks she would find
To dash her craft against, obliterate her mind.
Twisting in the wind, listing to one side,
Smashed to bits in the breakers,
she might save some pride.
A Captain always goes down
with her ship, you see …
What sweeter mercy could there be?

But you're my Anchorman! Hold me steady,
Steady as she goes, steady while she blows.
And I'll not fear the wind; I stand ready,
Ready with each roll, ready with my soul
To learn the ropes.

Useless Excuses that Keep You Down

What if and *If only* make a very dangerous game,
For these are wild wanderings
that never can be tamed:

These are questions that hide from answers,
they are thoughts with no good ends,
These are dodges from the *here and now*,
and they are *never, ever* friends.

What if and *If only* pack and peddle shame,
Seeking any quarry, to pin it with their blame.

Their ruse: to loose excuses, to
assign, and to condemn,
To duck responsibility, and make
sure you never mend!

No need to ask these questions, no need at all
There is nothing you can gain
by attending them at all.

What if and *If only* are a lot of useless gas,
For everyone on earth has a million possible pasts!

What use to second guess what
can't be changed in any way?
Look to your possible futures—
and start right now, today!

Loving who you are, right this very minute!
Putting your life in gear and pouring intention in it!

The Whole of Wealth

It's not how many and who
Love you.

Those are the wrong questions.

There is only one question:
Do you love yourself?

When you don't,
Nothing else helps.

When you do,
Nothing else hurts.

When you don't,
Nothing else works.

When you do,
Nothing else matters.

Surviving Fear

Everybody's Biggest Fear: The Imposter Syndrome

There is a dumb person inside my disguises
And if you found out, you would despise us:

The dumb person—the *real me*—
and all of my guises,
Faces, personas, costumes, and lies-es!

What would become then of all the devices
I maintain energetically to prevent this crisis?

Guess I would have to rewrite my song!
Lay down my worn-out disguises as wrong,

And out myself—here I am!—just my *self* alone,
And be authentic inside these bones,

And radiate the Spirit that indwells this loam
And somehow energetically be whole and at home.

Voices of Fear

What if I grow old, and no one wants me anymore?
What if I lose my beauty, and my
man goes out the door?
What if I'm not good enough just the way I am,
And must keep eagle eyes out for
blood-letting competition?

What if I must measure up to
some standard on high?
Or be sure of equally pleasing any and every guy?
What if I must measure up to some
standard down the street?
Or some standard in the workplace
so I can still compete?

Christine Van Brunt

What if I'm inconvenienced and
have to change my plans?
What if I get frustrated, or have
to work with my hands?
What if I can't buy enough for a
maintenance-free life?
What if my comfort's disrupted,
and there is stress or strife?

What if I can't laze around, and
really catch my breath,
Suspend all goals and activity?
Well isn't that like—Death?
What if, what if, what if: these fears *drive me the most*!
The *what if* parasites move in, and
they destroy their host.

Trust

That it will all happen, when it happens,
If it happens,
I happen to know

For goodness abounds us, surrounds us,
And grounds us;
And always is so.

To get it and net it and let it
Beget it,
Is what is the trick

Agreeing with seeing and being
And glee-ing
Is what makes us tick.

Perceive it, receive it, conceive it,
Believe it, oh,
Gush forth and grow

Manifest it, invest it, attest to it
Rest in it;
Make it your show

Your task but to ask, then simply
To bask is all
Ye need know

To sate, elate, emancipate,
Radiate is all
Ye need do

Behind and before and over and under
Your movie screen's
Action

Is the packable, stackable, implacable
Intractable
Law of attraction!

Conflicting Voices

Lies of You-Know-Who

Who tells you to get down on yourself?
I *know* who! The *Devil* do!
And *who* tells you to judge *everybody else?*
I *know* who! The *Devil* do!

Who tells you to get behind
The walls you make so you can't find
The things that give you peace of mind?
The Devil do!

He's a lying, sneaking, creeping, thieving thing …
And he wears pretty clothes so that
he don't look so mean …

Who tells you that you will fail?
I *know* who! The *Devil* do!
And *who* tells you, you *must turn tail?*
I *know* who! The *Devil* do!

Who tells you, you mustn't show,
And walls you in so you can't grow,
And feeds you lies so you won't know?
The Devil do!

He's a lying, sneaking, creeping, thieving thing…
And he wears pretty clothes so that
he don't look so mean…

Who tells you that it's too late?
You know who, the *Devil* do!
And who tells you that you don't rate?
You know who, the *Devil* do!

Who chains you to yesterday,
And serves up guilt three times a day,
And totals up a tally you can't pay?
The Devil do!

He's a lying, sneaking, creeping, thieving thing…
And he wears pretty clothes so that
he don't look so mean…

Voice of the Devil

Oh, I am the Devil…
I *seize* you from behind!
I seem on the level,
But I will *smite* your mind!

Shame and Blame are my real name
Though perfect my disguise;
I will have you hate yourself,
Without your getting wise!

I am the Devil…
My breath is in your ear;
My choke-hold's round your neck;
I prey upon your fear!

I'll ride you and I'll guide you,
You'll think you're in control…
When you hate others as yourself,
I'll have another soul!

Toe Holds in the Light

Voice of Truth

You are loved as you are, precious you!
Believe it and know it is true.

As blue loves the sky, and as grass loves the dew,
Love has its eye on you.

You are loved as you are, precious you!
Who else can manifest your truth?

The way that you glint with your energy print—
You alone. Only you. Exactly you.

Christine Van Brunt

Allowing Beauty

Refusal

I refuse to see it as a mess:
Abundant Life's prolificness!

Child Eyes

Oh for child eyes! Nature is awash
In what grownups call a mess,
All that glorious playfulness they too often
Count as trash—well, here's what I mean.

All that cottonwood is coming down
Again. Remember that magical stuff?
Those frightful hordes of Sunlit Fairies
In star-spangled tutus riding sideways on
The thermals through the whole high air,
—Stopping time—
—Glinting like miniature suns—
—In Slow
—Motion
—Giving the world a new shine—
Filling the entire atmosphere with
Tinker bell eagles, and
Diminutive puffed out sails?

Then drowning the grass with fluff?

It's like Winter has come again. But she
Forgot her beard, and couldn't look
So gruff. Disguised this time in
A summer gown, she snowed—
And is still snowing—
The softest, warmest down
Until all of the grown-ups say, "Enough!"

Here's what. I watched out my
Front door. And there was the
Landed fluff galore. And there was
A little chipmunk hugging the
Welcome mat in a lover's embrace
Gobbling up the weightless fuzz,
His little lithe body, all a-pulse,
Right on my front porch.

Don't talk anymore.
Don't tell about the work
And woe. Sit down.

Watch the show.

Losing the Day
for the Hours

Today and today and today
Hides—in this frantic race from hour to hour—
The Muse Invisible—drowned in the sound
And fury of our Butchered Time—

And she waits her moment upon the
stage. Out, out, shy Muse!
Wait not upon Time's rage! Nay, assume
The lead! Thrust forward thy truer nature—Quiet—
That the clanging gongs of our frayed nerves be

Stayed, and the ensuing Hush,
when all idiot noises drop
Away, summon our fractured spirits to a wider plane,
Where primordial silence calls up the depth and rush
Of purling currents in our soul's refrain.

Christine Van Brunt   230

In Praise of Slow Things

I like slow things: like summer days
  When the sky is white with haze

A bowl of sky the quiet pond
  Drone of bees on flower wand

Deep and slow the water's hymn
  Tolling bull-frogs on the rim

Dragonflies on unseen strings
  Hovering on soundless wings

Turtles torpid in the sun
On the rocks, their necks stretched long

The breathless breezes barely there
  Motionless the perfumed air

The snail who wears a striped shell
And leaves behind a silver trail

And every moment stretching long
The music of the Earth its song

To-Do List

Life's a list—
Things to do,
Things to buy,
Things you missed.

Did you know
That Old Father Freight Train Time—
Drumming, Thrumming, Thrumming, Thrumming
Day, Night, Night, Night,
Back, Forth, South, North,
Round and round your wound brain—is
Drowning out all Sound
And sawing the legs off
Wonder?

These mysteries—
New snowfall's hue,
Waking eyes,
Sacred trysts:
Like the cold flake on your tongue,

Cold's fresh shock to your warm, wet lung,
Each crisp, breath-taking beauty
In just about *all ordinary things*—
Break Time's bonds.

Pay Attention,
And they make
Still frames
Of silent, slow
Timelessness—
These things
That never make it to our lists:

Sloping branches
Draped in snow;
That tree you run past every day
Right now in your front yard is
Hugging the sky.

And I shouldn't wonder
If on this beautiful, bandaged morning
You were to wrap your arms around wonder
And throw your list away.

Jamaican Coffee

Black is the velvet, coating our tongues
Cleaving inside our cheeks and roof, oiling our gums
Invading our olfactories 'til we are tightly wound
Steeping all our senses in aroma that surrounds.

Black is the velvet swirling round and round
Oiling the smooth glide all the way down
From palate to stomach, rung by rung
Rich, full, and clinging, then cloying in our lungs.

Breathe deep the velvet of green rolling mountains,
Of fern, tree, and river, of earth, soil, and loam
Breathe deep the ocean that swaddles the island
Breathe deep the land this coffee calls home.

Breathe deep, Jamaica, her toiling people
Bunched biceps gleaming, blood, muscle, bone
Nut brown skin glowing, corded necks shining
Princely hearts canting, canting of home.

When you drink the coffee, and
it's warm in your hand
It's warm in your throat, and warm all the way down
Be one with the people, moving in union
'Tis a holy communion, oh drink their renown.

Christine Van Brunt

Regular Life

In so-called everyday ordinary things
There is luminous beauty,
—Which we so overlay with duty—
We become as birds who don't sing.

For instance, let me draw you a map:
What could be more clear
To the eye, more bell-like to the ear
Than *water,* running out of the tap?

Which every day occurs
—And it sings and it purrs—
And you can wash in it,
And drink it like that!

And while we're at it, for another instance
What could be more near
To the point, more relevant a career
Than that *needy insistence*

In your lap? That little person there
Who takes so much care
Is a *window*, you know,
Not a trap. Breathe him in like prayer.

Pay Attention

Every page of life is a fresh surprise
With trinkets to distract, perhaps to make wise

For the soul of the matter, best to test every guise
Every page of life is a fresh surprise

Apparent Disorder

Messes yield to incubations—
Incubations yield to emergence—
This is the way of all Beauty.

Assiduous appetite—Caterpillar,
Eating through leaves,
Foreruns the Chrysalis, dormant
In the eaves, foreruns the
Broken case, of the drying butterfly,
That soon will make a
Stunning flight.

The best things come from messes;
Out of messes come those things
Filled with the most clarity and light!

What is that substance seeds thrive in?
Dirt. And what comes out of it?
Flowers. Ferns. Leaves. Trees.

Christine Van Brunt

Things you can barely take your eyes from
In the Spring. Yes, dirt's the growing medium,
Along with rain and sun,
For the radiance of all
Living greenery.

And what has made the dirt, I wonder?
Aside from that profusion-of fallen leaves
Through which the snow has leached
All winter, and the rotting wood
Of our long dead trees?

We shun messes, and it's irrational,
For they are the work of God,
In a world of constant transformation.

And we are co-participants
In that work: for even messes of the heart
Can lead to clearer, brighter art.

The persistent, grainy sand, irritant supreme,
The tender oyster—pained—
Slimes and slimes again.

Toe Holds in the Light

Yes, down in that dark,
Closed place, here is
A pearl, whose luminous
Face, once exposed to light
Will shed infinite grace.

How is it that the brightest things
Are begotten in the dark?

What crushing forces,
Grinding tectonic plates,
Tons upon tons upon tons
Of weight
Will mold—from the "spent"
Carbon of decayed forests,
From the grime of sloughing,
Gritty coal—
The diamonds
That come alive in light?

Have no fear of messes.
Nor solitudes of
Gestations. These are not the chaos
You think.

Fear not the things that for beauty
Are the foundations!
Love them!
Up to the very brink—

Of some bright birthing yet to be
Some new awareness that makes you free.

Wait. Joyfully wait.
For what ethereal beauty—
Inside yourself,
Inside your home,
Inside your relationships,
Inside your life—
These forerunners will surely bring.
Not things to avoid,
These incubators of beauty!
When you find yourself in their midst,
—Sing!

Beauty, Beauty
Everywhere

Plates and Cups

Plates and cups
Are winking in cupboards,
Their shining surfaces
Stacked and aligned,

Waiting to reflect your life
And surroundings
As you reach them out of
Their prim confines.

They *play* with you
As you gingerly hold them
And transfer each carefully
To its tabletop place;

Note how they bend the light
As you move them,
To bunch up and stretch out
Your beautiful face!

Dish Bliss

What could be more tuneful
Than the tinkling water
As you fill the sink?
Or the whispering popcorn
Of rising suds?

Or the *ploosh* and *swash*
Of a sunken dish,
And the backfilling *slish*
Of the swirling water's
Incoming rush
To fill the displaced?

Nothing could.
Every beautiful thing
Lingers on
Behind itself,
Touches soft chimes
In the hearing mind.

Christine Van Brunt

What could be more silky
Than the sudsy soap
Slipping between
Your fingers and slicking
The dishes?

Or the curve
Of a smooth bowl
As around the inside
And outside
You chase the shine
In a losing race?

Nothing could.
Every beautiful thing
Unrolls out
Before itself,
Creates a ribbon of shine
In the soft silk of time
In the seeing mind.

Toe Holds in the Light

Boring or Soaring?

Sometimes, when you're worn out,
And life seems—well—boring,

Ask a different question,
Flip your perception.

Consider, might all this muck and mire
Make fertile ground for soaring?

Think about it for a minute,
Now that you are really in it.

Recognize—through the trappings—
How *Plenty* and *Scarcity* are mental wrappings,

Different faces on the same essence
That always rewards *attentive presence.*

For Joy, when not obvious on the face of things,
Often looms—balloons—in the deep of things.

It's worth the dive, don't you think?
Go ahead—while you're on the brink—

Take the drink.

Clean Sheets

I love clean sheets,
Hanging out on clotheslines:

White sails in the wind, snapping
Their wet, happy music, lifting
And curling, slapping and
Spreading as they dry.

Glowing geometry of curving planes—
Waving parallelograms
—Aligned in un-unison dipping and
Soaring, flowing around their mooring—
Tethered as they fly.

Sheer shimmering series of solitary wings
Furrowing and opening, billowing and blowing
Against the sky.

I love clean sheets,
Freighting up on air:

Their gentle, undulating genuflection
As they lose their damp,
And acquire their perfumed load of

Ozone, Bee-wings, Grasses,
Flowers, Moss, Earth,
Distance, Height, Sky, and Light,

Furling and lapping lazily in the sun,
Combing, caressing—swaddling the Tall Day—
With a flap and a sigh.

I love clean sheets,
After they come down:

Their snowy, luminous reams
—Like drifts from the Pleiades—
Mounded like soft vanilla creams,
Filling my nostrils with intoxicating scents.

These sunbathed swaths of cloth
—Soft as moths' wings, cool as air—
Will couch each precious head tonight,
Cradle each pulsing cell and limb,

Enfold each endlessly moving mind
In a seamless, starlit, silken womb,
And set them afloat, like so many boats,
In softly rocking rafts of dreams.

One Line at a Time

Every deliberate act,
Every spontaneous one,
Every behavior,
Every intention

Becomes a line
In your life-long poem.

Does it rhyme?
Does it flow?
Does it climb?
Will you know?

Are the lines structured or formless,
Disciplined or free,
As they wend their way
Out to sea?

Do they trip merrily
Like a mountain brook?
What will they unearth
In every nook?

Such a neat discovery
Every time
You get to add
Another line.

Wide Angles in Small Things

Collection

How many times have you admired
The speckles on a rock?
And thought of stars and galaxies
And just wanted to talk?

And talk and talk and talk about
What you saw on a walk?
Even past your bedtime when
It's time to change your socks?

Every beautiful thing on earth
Secretly unlocks
Inside your heart—in the deepest part—
A silver treasure box

Where every thing you ever saw
Is lovingly, carefully stored
And every thing you ever thought
Shines there, forevermore.

Toe Holds in the Light

Brief Eye Contact

Butterfly feet
Touch down
On a tremulous flower,
And pass a visible
Trembling power
Down the whole plant,
Whose genuflection
—Under their featherweight—
Is as brief as it is
Complete.

Oh, who could utter,
Who could even guess
That their tenuous power
As they barely press—
Would cause such
Tremor in
The bowing flower,
Such quiver in
The attending leaves,

Such shuddering
Down the whole stem
Setting even the roots
Aflutter?

No track there is
Of this brief meeting.
No records give away
The measure of
This moment, this

Fleeting brush
With a sacred Other.
The butterfly is gone,
The flower resprung;
But in the hush,

An impression indelible lingers on:
Eyes were met briefly;
But a whole
Soul feels
Known.

Unwritable Poem

The human foot—
Never sung,
Finely strung,
Lowest rung
On the whole weaving
Totem Pole
On which we stand—

Move, balance, glide—

Is a living poem
Of fluidity and grace.
Its support and structure,
Its range from stillness to mobility,
Its flexibility and strength

Coalesce …
To create, cushion …
And provide …

The entire ride

Of our lives.
Said foot daily
Displays an extensible
Array of moves:

From Subtlety—
Holding fast to uneven ground,
Able to grip it tightly,

To Grandiosity—
Moving vast lengths in sprints,
Or then again, in
Measured strides,

To Cleverness—
Performing feints and backups
Pivoting at our whim
In any direction.

A work of perfection
Is the foot.
If I declared it not,

I lied.

Who knew it packed
Twenty-six separate bones
—And among them formed
Thirty-three distinct joints
—Each moving separately—
Or in unison

As called for
By the changing demands
Of the terrain
Or their owner's
Moment by moment
Intention?

Who knew it took so many
Bones and joints—bundled with
Muscles, ligaments, and
Tendons—working together with
Tissues, nerves,
Arteries and
Veins—to create that resilient
Inaudible harmony
That moves us—
Continually
Reconfigured and aligned—

Aloft—
Forward, backward, or
Aside—

While we go unaware of their
Splendid craft, so
Soundlessly applied?

Until the foot is moot
Through injury or accident,

How many of us
Confront the magnitude
Of this mute and guileless
Glory on which we glide?

Or, when we do,
Which of us does not
With unutterable awe collide

Such as rattles the whole skeleton and
Shakes the very scales from our eyes?

To a Flower

Dear sight, flower bright
Pure statement of delight
Every day, every night
You grace our world with tender might.

Soft power, spreading bold,
Your seams are sewn with dusts of gold.
Though innocent of the hoard you hold,
The fragrance far the wind has told.

Bee wings buzz and sing,
Your golden stores the bees bring.
Hairy legs from your wealth will glean
A harvest fit for a bee-queen—

A harvest fit for a bee-queen
Who has rivers of honey in her dreams.
O'er the Earth her workers stream
To gather your pollen in, in reams.

Who knew such a vast domain
Comes of things smaller than seeds or rain?
Who knew when you unfurled
You'd unleash forces that feed the world?

Greeting

Goodbye, Sweet House! Hello, World!
All the fields with frost are pearled!

Morning lays her warming hand
All across the waking land.

Driving east is bliss for eyes;
I gaze on cloud-puffed, tufted skies.

Simple Words

Simple words are often best;
So, pack a wallop with a few.
Plainly tell, with heartfelt zest
What this moment, now, is true.

Here, Honey!
I love you.
I'm sorry.
Come rest.
Mommy!
Watch me!
Good morning!
I did my best.

My pleasure!
Look what I did!
How can I help?
Thank you.

Have a good time!
We're rooting for you!
See you later.
I need you.

Flipped Perspective:
Grave to Cradle

You could say the old woodpile
Outside our kitchen window
Is a pile of junk. It has been there a long time,
Has lost its usefulness for stove wood,
Is too rotted through.

But those loose lying relics of decay
Are open arms, embracing life. For
Under your eyes, these seemingly
Passive logs burst into squirrels
Like so many gray flames.
They break into chipmunks
Like so many striped comets.

And underneath this beautiful outer dance
Is a secret inner dance.

Toe Holds in the Light

These decomposing logs
Are busy tenement houses.
Are criminal dens.
Are safe harbors.
Are incubators.
Are laboratories of chemical reconfigurations.
Are on their way to becoming fertile earth.

This old woodpile is a front
For a vast series of underworld operations,
Hidden from your eyes
Unless you look.
Under the loosening bark
—In the spongy
Yellow and orange interior—
Seditions are taking place.
Gangs—each wearing their gang colors—
Are fencing their stolen goods,
Turning logs into loam.

Christine Van Brunt   272

This old woodpile is shelter to
hundreds of shy species
Going about their quiet work in the dark.
God's work:
Making daily resurrections,
Transforming dead wood
To living soil
Where Life itself
Teems and thrives.

Inside the crumbling logs' soft
Warm womb, small life forms gestate,
Keeping—in their tiny huge way—
The permanence
Of Death
At bay.

My Bride's Eye

Can you see in my bride's eye,
In the glimmer of that deep brown pool,
The trout that rises to the fly?

In my bride's eye, can you see
In the murmur that swells to a torrent of love
The breeze that flutters the canopy?

Can you see in my bride's eye,
In the ripple of that singing brook,
The teeming life go rollicking by?

In my bride's eye, can you see
In the dappling sun of that shady glade
The flower bowing under the bee?

Can you see in my bride's eye,
In the sparkle larger than bigger things,
The curve of the earth and the arc of the sky?

Inexpressible, but I will try
To tell all I see—from cell division
To galaxies—in my bride's eye.

Love Listens

Loss

I wish I had listened more
And talked less,
Had asked more questions,
Given fewer explanations,

Had heard the
Heart and stir
Behind your words,

Had listened for
The faint murmur
Of what was not said.

I wish, instead of frantically catching
You up on the whole inside of my head,
I had followed up on the glimpses
Of the inside of your precious head

That I had recognized—
Paid attention to—
The moments in our conversation
When you—

Were poised

To reveal

Your

Self.

Limerick for a Listening Friend

I have a dear and forever friend
Who listened through my story, end to end.
She brought her two ears,
Her heart, and no jeers—
Treasures beyond measure. I thank her. Amen.

If Children Were Perfect Orators

If children were perfect orators,
They would never whine,
While wheeled around in stores
Overtired and confined.

Instead they might say, "Hey,
Y'know, I'm all tuckered out.
I feel out of control, and am,
So can you help me out?"

"Of a triggering event
I need to make you aware,
But you aren't hearing me at all,
And it seems a bit unfair."

"I know you're very busy,
But I'm tired and stressed too.
Can you take some time for me?
How many more things do we have to do?"

"I'm feeling disappointment
For a decision that you made,
But more than that I'm frustrated
I can't rest *or* participate!"

"My feelings are *so big*,
I don't know how to let them out!
If I knew a better way,
I wouldn't whine or spout."

"Please help me with my feelings,
Walk in my shoes and share;
I'm feeling so invisible,
And I need you to care."

"You know what hurts the most?
I just want to be seen.
Understood. Cared about.
By one who's not so mean."

Toe Holds in the Light

If children were perfect orators,
    They would never whine;
If parents were perfect listeners
Would children have to whine?

Love Listens

Love, love, love, and listen. Listen.
Truths for you chime and twirl and glisten!

Moment by moment, place by place,
Soul by soul, face by face.

Love, love, love, and listen. Listen.
Truths for you jiggle and pop and glisten!

Sound by sound, sight by sight,
In music, in silence, in darkness, in light.

Love, love, love, and listen. Listen.
Truths for you whisper and tap and glisten

Where *Joy* and *Peace* are states of mind
Everywhere their lease, *Always* their time.

Your hand, your eye, your supple skin
Hold wonders so vast from your cells to the rim

Of the universe and to imagination's limit.
How far out does it go? How deep can we plumb it?

Forever it goes, these works of perfection.
Forever, on each hand, in every direction.

Love, love, love, and listen. Listen!
Truths for you knock and open and glisten,

Sing and glisten, glisten and sing,
Sing the song of Everything.

Missy Doodle Dorothy

Missy Doodle Dorothy, my best friend
Her right ear a friend did lend
Listened long and listened deep
Missy Doodle Dorothy, keep, keep, keep.

Missy Doodle Dorothy used her rope
Belayed a novice up a slope
Dorothy's arm and Dorothy's skill
Gave the novice dare to will.

To the Listener

Your voice is golden as a sweet oil balm;
Its liquid drops slip in my fevered ear,
And pain subsides … A quiet hand appears
O'er quivering strings, sets down a palm …

Out from my soul comes an answering calm,
Where trembled my chords before
with notes too shrill,
And your low tones enfold me and hold me still;
Palpable salvation steeps me in psalm.

Out from the soul-soothed hush, your smiling eyes,
Find—then my demons crush—with lullabies,
Soaking my soul in peace, which swells to song!

Oh, keep I in my heart *what dwelleth* here
Which sweeps away debris of every dissonant tear …
With my own bell tones I'll ring
the air, my whole life long.

Hello, Fellow Climbers

Man Eaten Alive in Partnership Dance

The man is like good hardwood
—Solid, steady, strong—
Enduring, good to build with,
Never breaks down,
Lasts long.

Inside his rough bark
Is all pith and prayer and heartwood
—Resilient, guileless, and good—
So quiet about where he's been hacked,
Perhaps misunderstood.

The woman is as fire:
A thousand shapes of light,
Her golden feet all swishing motion,
Flowering the night,
Her ruby fingers swimming air,
Red birds in flight,

Her lips, kisses hissing,
Whining in the night,
Her breath in wisps,
Whispering
Low moaning into might.

Hold her still—she'll burn you
Enclose her—she'll die out
But worse it is to spurn her
You'll yearn 'til you cry out

So be as fuel; allow
The large bites of you she'll take
You'll be repaid in full
By the dance
The noise
The warmth
The light
The life
You two will make.

My Three Sons

I have three sons,
And there is a castle,
—A whole country—
In my heart for each one.

They are bone of my bone
And flesh of my flesh,
And my heart is their home,
And my heart is their nest.

I get to kiss a bruised pride,
Brush a tousled head,
Squat down side by side
For bugs, living or dead.

Am I raising them,
Or are they raising me?
If you looked us over,
What would you see?

I have three sons
And more rich could not be!
What would you trade
So you could be me?

Beloved Friends

My beloved friends,
You are as the brightest moon
To my darkest nights.

Love Song to Our Aged Ones

Your eyes are rimmed with wrinkles;
They're dimming with the time.
You think they are ugly;
To me they look so fine.

In your gray head you know things
That I don't understand:
Your fingers, they have stiffened;
Yet you have such gentle hands.

I see the milk of wisdom
In your cloudy eyes;
I have often wondered
What goes on beyond your sighs.

In your vast heart, you've felt things
That I have yet to know,
And I would gladly trade my youth
For the kindness that you show.

She is a Saint, Marjory

She is a saint, Marjory,
Though she sees it not.

These two—who rail at her
guidance again and again—
Trail through her patience, leaving
their tracks on all that she's got,

Their handprints on every span of space
that she would have clean—
Presumptuous glee! Laughing and
free! Because they know haven.
They know she's the one—when they're
broken or torn—who can mend;
And yet they try her, and test her, and
wrest away all that they can.

Commotion shows like trampled snow
Where a Saint has been.

She is a saint, Marjory,
Though she knows it not.

These two, tucked into their
dreams, by her loving hands,
Are at utter peace now, these little
rapscallions, who so lately fought.

Now, their hair on their pillows is
softly spread like an open fan,
As though it were blown ever so
faintly by a kissing wind.

Their plump cheeks are untroubled
now, as they breathe out and in,
Content as those at rest who live life to the brim.

The Quiet tells as loud as bells
Where a Saint has been.

Love Song to All Stroke and Alzheimer's Patients

Your life is a gift to me, even
though to you it's weary;
You're the Sharpening Stone, and I'm the Knife …
And the edge you're putting on me
is an edge of keener love,
But always being rubbed on must be pretty rough,
Pretty rough.

Silence is a whirlwind, hurling
round the thoughts within,
You can't even say the things you feel …
There's an old Bible story in the Book of Job;
It was out of a whirlwind, God almighty spoke,
God spoke.

Stillness is a Teacher, and her lessons are all hard,
But in the learning is reward …
For the heart that will not still itself,
can never know God's love.
It's when the heart is still, we feel God move,
Feel God move.

You are learning to receive; I am
learning more of serving—
Helpers for each other's deepest need …
You always did for others! Now let me do for you!
For Love is never bothered; it's constantly renewed,
Ever new.

Perfection and Deformity, Hand in Hand

Perfection and Deformity are mighty friends;
They sashay down the street, holding hands.
Undisturbed when stuff hits the fan,
Unperturbed. Ain't it grand?

To My Missionary Sister

I see you in Africa,
And I know you:
Lady of the St. Vrain River,
Lady of American streets:
Richmond, Philadelphia, Chicago, Ventura,
Lady of crop walks, mountain streams,
Highways and byways, cities and small towns,
Lady of babies and beginnings:
"See how he loves you," you cooed
To the mom who was tired and scared and new.

I see you in Africa,
But I saw you here too:
Lady of people, one-on-one tutor;
"Good reading," you smiled
To the tentative child.
I see you always, always wading in,
To mountain cold, to tropical heat,
To thick, to thin,
I see you wading in.

Christine Van Brunt

I see you in Africa,
Giving and tired,
Singing and triumphant,
With your husband holding hands.
I see you beside the still waters.
I see you walking by the river,
Walking between villages
—In the warm snow of white butterflies—
Walking overland.

Wherever you choose
To spend your days,
Your ripples spread out forever.
Africa is not big enough
To hold your love;
Here in our heartland
I am lapped by its waves.

And that ocean between us
Is folding and rolling
Repeating and tolling
Its booming refrain:
Love saves.

Danger in the
Unexplored

Heart in My Throat

This is a voice for Matthew's Mother:
What she wants—but doesn't know how—to say
To her newly enlisted eighteen-year-old son:

My tall, grown-up, handsome son
I can't think of anything harder to do
Than saying good-bye to you

And I'm no good at it. The love I have for you
Is so strong it hurts. From dusk to dawn it aches,
And I don't always say or do

The things you like, or even things
That I like, or even things that *make sense*–
Even from my own point of view!

Heck, I'm just trying to stay relevant
To a life that is all grown-up and
yet still so new. And I get
Irrational about the most minor things.

I know that I do. And I'm sorry too.
And I see myself losing it, and still I can't stop,
Like I'm wound up too tight, helpless

To help you. Not that you want it, but it
Troubles me that I don't know
how to do that anymore.
It's dumb, I know, but I feel helpless and stupid

And so sad and confused! And so everything
Turns into an earthshaking fuss, almost like how else
Do I express that I love you this much?

It feels so new to me, this saying good-bye to you.
I didn't realize it would come so
soon. I don't feel ready.
I guess a mom never does. I
worry I haven't given you

Enough exposure or wisdom or—
whatever moms do—
Haven't said all that could be
said, really equipped you
For what's coming ahead.

Christine Van Brunt   308

You are so well prepared in so
many ways, but—well—
Still so young, and I can't help
wondering some, when you
Walk out that door, does that mean,

We're done? Will we still sit at the kitchen table
And just talk sometimes, when you come home?
(If you come home?)

I'm scared because we lack the time
I'm sorry because I lack the skill to tell you
How terribly proud I am of you

And how I always will care so much about
What you are doing and how it's going
And is it okay or rough? I know you're

Tough, but I'm not so much.
Here's what I'd say if I knew the words:
I'm so bursting proud of you

It makes me crazy; I love you deeper than the ocean.
And here are the things I'm worried about,
Dear, and I need to tell you about them

To feel like a good mother, so may I spell them out?
And here are the things I need to say and
then I'll be getting out of your way
But honey, no matter where you
go or what you achieve—

And I know you'll be achieving marvelous things!—
I'll still be your Mom. You know what I mean?
And I'm just a bit lost in the fears and worries

That are the curse and prerogative of being a mom.
The problem is I need a hug. And the problem is
Not you, but me, my Son.

Voice of an Addiction

No, you can't saw off my leg. I don't
Care that it is swollen and
Purpled with gangrene.

I'm not through with it yet.
See what I mean?

How can you be so mean?
Telling me to live with just a stump?
Don't you *feel anything*?

I don't care that the sickly thing
Has me thrashing all night
And reeling all day—

I'm used to it, don't you see.

I can't even tell any more
What's the leg
And what's me.

You say it drags me down,
Threatens my whole being.

Can't you hear what I say?
Can't you see what I'm seeing?

I can't see living without it.
You want to take it?
Then take me.

'Druther you cut off my life,
And let me just keep the leg.

Ageless Is Love

Slow Cooking

A family
Can be savory, slow-cooked fare.
First, the base is chosen
With splendid care,
And stews and simmers awhile
Scenting the air.

Then, one at a time, each
Pristine ingredient is
Lovingly received, lovingly
Prepared, cherished for its perfect
Wholeness and completeness, and
Gratefully added.

Each goes in—fresh and bright and raw—
Perfect and whole and beautiful
Exactly as it is—
Imparting its own color and texture and zest
—Offering its personality to the pot—
Swapping around with all the rest.

Toe Holds in the Light

Then warmth, gently applied
Over a very long period of time,
Helps each ingredient work a magic on the others
That couldn't be worked any other way,
Until, truly, the Whole is more than the
Sum of its Parts. Such are the cooking arts.

The nourishment? Unparalleled.
The flavor? Sumptuous.
The comfort? I'm telling you.
And there's gravy too.

Father Time

Father Time never minds his job,
keeping one thing from another;
He collapses things inside the heart,
and joins them there forever.

Greedily he scoops them up—
events involving brothers—
To swim, like tadpoles, in his cup,
and be preserved forever.

He takes the sun, the dappled grass,
the bright Potomac River—
He can place them under glass, and
make them yours forever.

He makes a globe—around it
goes—spin it on your finger
Things stream by, you hold them nigh,
you hold them nigh forever.

Today is now so far away from that day by the river,
But on this blue road, o'er this blue
bay, the sky so bright it shivers,

Father Time has reversed time;
I'm back beside the river—
Backlit by the scudding clouds of
gray and slate and silver—

Where our sons frolicked in the sun
(Time holds them there forever),
Today, far flung—but in here hung—
as they hung then, together.

Hear the mandolins they strummed,
the chorus of the water …
Know in all of Christendom no more
content a mother and father.

Annals of Love

I love so when you come
With all your bright youth,
Current knowledge,
Complex circuitry
Of interests!

You dazzle us
With your speed,
Your intellects,
Your depth.

You catch us up
In your fountains
Of up-surging energy—
Flumes catching the light!

You stimulate us in dozens of
Simultaneous ways, sharing:
Movies, shorts, songs, satires
Workouts, games, conversations, ideas

And the streaming days
Gurgle and flow:
All interleaving patterns
—Moving and heaving—
Starting as rapids that roar
—Spray kicking high—
And when there's time,
If we're not rushed,
Swirling as eddies that circle
And quietly sigh,
And then if there's even more time,
—White unplanned spaces—
Pooling in places,
Deep and slow.

Watch my heart, I must!
But I always forget to.
Year after year after year
It feels like we have forever
When you're here …
To explore and play and trust
And take time to know …

Because you animate our whole
Movie screen,
You and your movable show.

And then, you go.

Let Me Really See You

Let me really see you before you go
Let me always tell you so you always know
How much I love you

Every time you enter a room
My molecules know. There is so much of Home
In being with you.

You vibrate the air. Like a secret bell
You slip into my consciousness. My every cell
Senses, salutes you.

The utter rightness of having you near
Makes me so want you to always be here
With me, where I am—

If you so choose, because in ways
I can't name, you somehow complete me.
I'll never be the same.

Even when you're *not doing a thing*
I want to be around, *lest I miss anything*
—I love being with you.

Innocent of your impact, you are how
I want to be: to *be like Home* for people
The way you *are Home f*or me

So stay, if you will, and if you can
May your time on earth coincide
With my span

Stay. It is so good, your being here
Don't let it be the other way.
Stay. And if not, then …

Let me really see you before you go
Let me always tell you so you always know
How much I love you.

Remembering

Do you remember
When we were young, honey?
And you loved me
With all your might?

And I would pick wildflowers
And put them all over the house
In bottles and jars,
Anything I could find?

And we held hands
And ran around to farm auctions
And small towns
All over the countryside?

And we had so much energy
We could head home
To see our parents four states away,
And we could drive all night?

I remember too.
I so love you.

Christine Van Brunt

More Than You Even Know

As little ones, most of your love was unconscious;
It was so bound up in survival and comfort,
—Being held, jounced, carried—you
could not see me as "other."
I was that wonderful or terribly necessary "Mother."

As two-year-olds, most of your love was contentious
Because you were enjoying the
grand discovery that *You*
Were Not Me, and it was precious fun to pull away,
Say "No," and—when you were
feeling safe—go your own way.

As six-year-olds, most of your love was exuberant,
Bounding with tugs and hugs, talks and treasures.
I was your gym mat, piggy-back-rider,
ally to your expanding span,
Party-hatcher, story-fountain, and number one fan.

As teens, most of your love was
private and self-conscious
Because it was so bound up in the
important task of separating
—So you could unfold and
become your own entity—
I became—you had to see me—mainly as enemy.

As young men, you speak generously of your love,
Your adult eyes glimpsing me as a real human being
—With no godlike powers to threaten or fix—
Who poured thought—but mostly
love—into the mix.

You offer degrees of tolerance, amused affection.
It's delightful to me to be seen more as I am, and
To see myself anew through your lenses too.
Thanks for bringing me along, your toddling Mom.

You may not be able to see it now,
But with every layer of life experience you add,
You will love me more deeply than you can now.
You may protest, but don't; this isn't bad.

One day, when you hold one of your own,
More love for me will sing in your bones.
One day, when your heart is in your throat
As one goes off to middle school on a tentative note,

One day, when you wave as they go out the door,
And you don't know what's next or if there's more,
You'll know me better than you do now;
You'll remember me kindly, with a kindly brow.

And the full extent of your love you'll realize
Only after I've passed on. And not
one iota should that worry you.
Just press on. A wonderful thing about love is
Its full extent is *never* reached. As long as you live,
It keeps adding on ...

Brimming with
Thanks

Moved

A friend of mine saw the Mona Lisa,
And that was when he cried...
His wife saw the Code of Hammurabi,
And that was when she cried...
I saw a model of the human spinal column,
And that was when I cried.

If we knew but a fraction of that which we've got,
Or even an atom thereof,
We'd stop in our tracks—our mouths agape—
To ponder the power of such stuff!
Imagine engineering such a flexible structure
That so subtly and precisely moves!

Could we enumerate the remarkable things
That move us in pivotal ways,
Our lips would continually have to give thanks,
Our spirits offer up praise.
In this finite life, there's not enough time
For all the thanks we could say.
Might as well let it exude from our pores;
Might as well start today.

Remembering Haiti

For the unshaken earth I woke up to today,
For the roof that was still in place over my head,
For the things small and great
that were going my way,
Like I found myself safe and snug in my bed,

That my front door would open,
and my yard was still there,
That wherever I looked I could assume I'd find
Mugs in the cupboards, cushions on chairs
My car in the driveway, the road just behind,

That when I left for work, I knew
work would be there,
And I could have water and coffee and food,
And could climb between floors on workable stairs,
And walk between walls on floors that were good,

It seems plain as a shot going off in my head,
To give thanks for what's mainly unseen and unsaid.

Christine Van Brunt   332

Stirrings

Nothing makes for reveries
More than yonder poplar trees;

The way they sway so in the wind
Hearkens to my heart within.

All the leaves in constant motion
—Quaking as with deep devotion—

Are twinkling stars upon the trees
Rifled by each playful breeze.

Nothing in the trees is still;
How they dance and always will.

So my soul is ever full,
Dances too, and feels the pull,

Of the same force in the stir.
Small wonder: same choreographer.

I Would Give You Yellow

May buttercups spring up in crowds,
And daffodils fill your eyes
May happy thoughts arise in clouds
Like yellow butterflies

May forsythias—their ruffled arms—
Embrace the bluest sky
And needle-swift goldfinches
Sew yellow as they fly

May corn on the cob, bursting sweet
Foretoken paradise
May your two lips and tongue and teeth
Be washed in lemon pies.

May yellow hearth fire sing and dance
The warmth within your door
And yellow kittens joust and prance
Across your soul's wide floor.

For you are warm as yellow
A sun on fields of dew
A friend in every weather
And I am glad for you.

Toe Holds in the Light

Belly to Belly with the Good Earth

Belly to belly with the good earth!
Nose in the grass, nose in the dirt!
Sniffing its fragrance, hugging its girth!
It's good to be alive!

Hugging the bark of the sycamore tree,
Shinnying up its majesty;
Scratches on arms will *not stop* me!
It's good to be alive!

Up in her heights I freely stand—
All the backyard in my command!
Communing with Sky in this moving land!
It's good to be alive!

Christine Van Brunt

At The Summit

Love Chant

Woman, I love you.
I love you as the sun loves the grass.

Your sweetness hangs in the air
Slips into every breeze
Fills my nostrils and lungs
Until drunken,
I sink to my knees
Take you in my hands
Breathe deeply of you
My nose in your softest places.

You are like sweet, fruited earth!
Small and compact as you are,
None of my span
Could contain your perfume's
Girth; I strive with the
Strength of my sinews
To hold and contain
Something too subtle
Even for the finest of nets.

Instead I am contained
Oh, soft fragrance
In the demure of your
Depths; I am senseless with your
Scents; where I dumbly command
It is I who am commanded.
In your dominion,
Utterly helpless I am.

I surround you,
Press to your core
I enfold you—ever wanting more—
And I am helpless,
Helplessly yours,
Inhaling you
Such that I lose my breath
And now is forever
And forever is now
And the wonder and why of it
Overcomes how

And all the power and glory
Of any prowess I possess
Crawls in the bottomless thrall
Of your gleaming tress,
And flesh, and face—
I give such as I have,
I give it all.

And at last, supine, I lie in the sun
And commit as I have never done
To inhale
Your sweetness forever,
Woman,
I love you.

Woman I love you
I love you as the sun loves the grass.

Come Let Us Romp Round The Universe Together

Come let us romp 'round the universe together
Loving it all with an up-surging love
Seeing the beauty in each cell and atom
Outpouring the beauty that in us does move!

Come let us shine with a bottomless radiance
Pouring forth energy in endless supply:
Unstoppable streams that wend around boulders
Unstoppable heights as vast as the sky!

Why does the bud push up through the darkness
Moving toward light that it cannot yet see?
Why is the flower such a powerful magnet
So loved and sought and caressed by the bee?

How is each dewdrop its own little ocean?
How is each dewdrop its own little sun?
How does it tell with its wee tiny beauty
Of things that are so large they touch everyone?

See all the world sing with life's happy music!
Joyfully *Seasons* sling messy array!
Life calls to Life for a myriad of reasons
And *Nature is always and ever at play*!

Creating and loving and heaving and birthing
Lush new delights–whether anyone sees!
Some live a day like the gossamer mayfly
Some live for ages like the turtle and tree

Seen and unseen, *Life* gushes beauty
Such is her nature and ever will be
Let us rejoice in her rich happy tumult
And join the expansion of *Life's Jubilee*!

Toe Holds in the Light

Under the Canopy

Under the canopy of silk and light
Airily fluttering and gleaming white

A shining eye—with heart and will—
Smiles at her guy, and the world goes still.

His hand she keeps; she swings her arm!
She fairly leaps with spirit warm!

His parents are moved to see their son
So well beloved, so happily won!

And they are almost overcome.

The occasion here: its what and why
Is complete and clear in her bright eye

The trees all swoon—bowing, swaying—
The bride and groom their vows are saying

Christine Van Brunt

And only this (the people fade)
Is all there is (in the quiet glade)

The couple's bliss, their elation high
Betold by this: A bride's brown eye

And how he can love her so—his parents—
Now hers too—know why.

Homecoming

In ways beyond any human tongue
The errand was a happy one
As we flew west from near to far
We knew every second how lucky we were
To welcome home our son from war.

We were constantly cognizant that
Many other parents wouldn't have that—
The welcome on the homeward shore
The welcome each has waited for
To have a son come home from war.

Grins were anatomical to our faces
Couldn't have been washed off
or slapped off, yet traces
Of poignancy accompanied our joy
We wished it could be for every boy
To be the son come home from war.

He had known the risk and so had we
And he had accepted it graciously
And so had we, I mostly thought,
But if the shoe were on the other foot—
And our huggable son would come no more—

—That thought we didn't dare to think
—That thought we couldn't help but think
—The possible futures we kept at bay
—The things we carefully didn't say
Had our dear one been among the dying—

We were committed to that certain grace
To show dignity and a brave face
To hold fast the honor, the meaning of service
And the terribly real and valued purpose—
There'd be the rest of our lives for crying.

His homecoming almost too joyful to bear!
From that other fate we were gratefully spared!
So grateful were we to stand in the throng
Wives dressed to the nines—new babies along—
Beaming and waving and shouting our bliss

Now three hundred men, alive and tall
In cammies and covers one and all
Which one? Which one? Oh, the thrall!
In that beautiful sea, feeling so small
Oh, my god, there he is! There he is! There he is!

The crying, the contact, the look in his eyes
He's whole and he's here and you still recognize
The same boy you raised, he still has that grin
Even though you only come up to his chin
Tears, laughter choke your throat and your breast
And your boy is clasping you to his chest.

Still Life

On summer evenings, fresh with leaves,
When green wands criss-cross
And wreathe the eaves,

And silent bushes along neighborhood streets
Hang heavy with blossoms
And their odors release

I'm compelled out of doors, simply cannot stay in,
The whole swelling Earth
Calls my blood like kin.

The world is still. The darkening trees
Make moving silhouettes
In the gloaming breeze

And the whole fragrant Night is alive and hovering
And hangs there, hushed
Like a lover, listening

And the bluing sky, fading into night,
Seems a lullabye
And a holy rite

And the satin air, tracing my skin
Is a zephyr fair
That folds me in

And the arms of trees, as they drape the night
Hug the whole high air
With all their might

Oh Night, hanging quietly over all,
So still, I quiver
In your scented thrall

I've seen your pageantry before
Felt your majesty
At my soul's door

Yet awhile longer, Dear Night, keep me
Let my mortal heart
Pump eternity.

Christine Van Brunt

350

Imagining the Voice of God

I am the force of growing plants;
I am the chemistry of ants;
I am the sun's warm, piercing lance
O'er all the Earth.

I am the bruise in the human heart;
I am the muse for all your art;
I will always take your part;
I know your worth.

I am the depth inside your groans;
I am all your rods and cones;
I am the Source inside your bones,
Genesis and Birth.

Home Invasion

Love is large.
Large enough to
Swaddle
All.

You.
Me.
Earth.
Universe.
Multiverse?

All.

Yet, fine enough to
Enter
All.

Pollen
Molecule
Atom
Quark

Christine Van Brunt

All.

To move through us and in us
Illuminating our beautiful selves,
And connecting us with

All.

LIVE

listen|imagine|view|experience

AUDIO BOOK DOWNLOAD INCLUDED WITH THIS BOOK!

In your hands you hold a complete digital entertainment package. Besides purchasing the paper version of this book, this book includes a free download of the audio version of this book. Simply use the code listed below when visiting our website. Once downloaded to your computer, you can listen to the book through your computer's speakers, burn it to an audio CD or save the file to your portable music device (such as Apple's popular iPod) and listen on the go!

How to get your free audio book digital download:

1. Visit www.tatepublishing.com and click on the e|LIVE logo on the home page.
2. Enter the following coupon code:
   8aee-d614-9ede-f5ed-c4bf-a8e3-31b2-5a4e
3. Download the audio book from your e|LIVE digital locker and begin enjoying your new digital entertainment package today!